ADRIAN GILPIN

Adrian Gilpin is Chairman of the Institute of Human Development and Chairman of the Transformational Leadership Forum.

He runs a regular series of public programmes that coach individuals through the thinking skills and attitude shifts that make them unstoppable.

His speaking appearances on international business platforms attract high praise for his motivating message and his passionate style. He regularly speaks on:

- Building Unstoppable Teams
- Communicating with Passion, Power and Precision
- Unstoppable Leadership – The Emerging Power
- Building your Vision and Making It Happen

Adrian also consults to large organisations that are implementing core transformation, and entrepreneurial businesses that dream of being the best in their field.

He continues to lead the Institute of Human Development through its rapid expansion as it takes its place as a major European centre of excellence in the coaching of human potential.

What they say about Adrian Gilpin's Seminars & Lectures

'Of immense value to reaffirm my beliefs and spark-off thoughts to creating new beliefs'
MARTIN PARKER, SBC WARBBURG

'Made me ask questions of myself that I would rather not ask'
LISA CHRISTMAS, COMMUNICATIONS PROJECT

'. . . a very powerful and significant presenter . . . These were the three most important days of my life . . . I feel privileged to have enjoyed the course in the early days of IHD with the dynamic, compassionate leadership of Adrian in a small group, with his availability for personal clarification, his incisive skill at reasoning out the essential points and his awareness of interest in where people are at'.
MARY SPREADBURY (ULAC/PPEC/BTVC)

'Clear, inspiring, intriguing – opened my eyes to a whole new way of looking at things.'
MICHAEL SMITH, PARTNER, GIL TURNER & TUCKER SOLICITORS

'This was a phenomenally powerful programme from which I have learned a tremendous amount about my make up and why I am who I am, which is a question that I wanted to know for years.'
PETER MCIVOR, BARTERCARD

'The best U.K. presenter I have seen.'
VALERIE CAMP – ESSENTIALS FOR HEALTH

'Done NLP. Done Tony Robbins. For me, Adrian Gilpin's approach is the logical and more powerful next step. Powerful. Honest. Open. Genuine.'
JOHN DONNELLY, MANAGING DIRECTOR, LEARNING POINT & MASTER
PRACTITIONERS NLP

'A star is born'.
PAUL PINNOCK, OPERATIONS MANAGER, THE NATIONAL MARITIME MUSEUM

'Excellent. He was inspirational. Certainly one of the best, if not the best, I have ever attended.'
VIVIEN WOODGER, PERSONNEL MANAGER, STONE INTERNATIONAL

'Well structured . . . Thought Provoking . . . Excellent . . . Adrian Gilpin opened the door to what can be achieved and how to achieve it.'
SUE WULFF, QUALITY MANAGER, KENT TEC

'Very, very powerful.'
TONY HERBERT, PRINCIPAL COMMUNICATIONS LTD

'Thoroughly inspirational . . . entertaining, humorous, considerate and enlightening. It exceeded my expectations.'
IAN GEORGE, GENERAL MANAGER, HERITAGE PROJECTS LTD

UNSTOPPABLE PEOPLE

*How ordinary people achieve
extraordinary things*

ADRIAN GILPIN

C

CENTURY
BUSINESS

This edition first published by Century Ltd
Random House, 20 Vauxhall Bridge Road,
London SW1V 2SA

Random House Australia (Pty) Limited
20 Alfred Street, Milsons Point, Sydney,
New South Wales 2061, Australia

Random House New Zealand Limited
18 Poland Road, Glenfield,
Auckland 10, New Zealand

Random House South Africa (Pty) Limited
Endulini, 5A Jubilee Road, Parktown 2193, South Africa

Random House UK Limited Reg. No. 954009

A CIP catalogue record for this book is available from the British Library

Papers used by Random House UK Limited are natural,
recyclable products made from wood grown in sustainable forests.
The manufacturing processes conform to the environmental
regulations of the country of origin.

ISBN 0 7126 7808 5

Typeset by MATS, Southend-on-Sea, Essex
Printed and bound in Great Britain by
Mackays of Chatham PLC, Chatham, Kent

Companies, institutions and other organizations wishing to make bulk
purchases of any business books published by Random House should
contact their local bookstore or Random House direct:
Special Sales Director
Random House, 20 Vauxhall Bridge Road,
London SW1V 2SA
Tel 0171 840 8470   Fax 0171 828 6681

CONTENTS

For Francesca

Acknowledgements

There is one name on the front of this book and yet many people who have created it. My first thanks must go to Jonathan Langdale whose seemingly endless, patient hours of listening to me talk about the experiences which have shaped this tale were rewarded with even longer hours spent mapping out the structure of the book, taking my rambling thoughts and rugged words and sculpting them into meaning and coherence. Jean Brigg, my personal assistant, endured all of my frustrations and moods while I made a vain attempt to run a business as I struggled with ideas, words, manuscripts and computers. My friends and colleagues have given me so much intellectual and moral support during the last extraordinary five years, particularly John Sarson who keeps me on target; Celia Gray, Hilary Davies and Nick Bruce who spent many hours challenging my logic with disarming honesty while I developed our early seminars; John Donnelly who keeps giving me work and making me laugh; Melanie Pettman whose creative genius keeps me right at the edge of my own comfort zones; Tony O'Connell whose passion for language and leadership keep us both distracted from earning a living; my clients, so many of whom become real friends, and the countless others whose confidence in me has given me a new experience of life, business and myself over the past five years. Simon King and Elizabeth Hennessy at Random House have allowed me to deliver a book that bears no resemblance to the original treatment. Their quiet confidence has made my debut completely painless.

My last word of thanks, though, must go to my wife Francesca whose faith is beyond anything I have experienced with another being; she has given me the courage to trust myself, she has inspired me to explore new ideas, new ventures and a new me, and she has given me the ultimate gift of love and bliss, a family – Sophie, Phoebe and Charlie whose glorious minds and shining spirits are the wind beneath my wings.

PREFACE

*We are like dwarfs on the shoulders of giants, so that we
can see more than they, and things at a greater
distance, not by virtue of any sharpness of sight on our
part, or any physical distinction, but because we are
carried high and raised up by their giant size.*

BERNARD OF CHARTRES C. 1120 AD

A man on a long journey came to a desert. The sand burned his feet like
fire. There was no shade and the sun burned down upon his head.
There was no water. 'If there is no water,' he said to himself, 'then I
must remain here, or return to my old country.' Behind him lay the
wilderness where he had wandered for many days, and he had no
longing for the old country any more. Beyond the desert lay the only
chance of finding the home he desired.

He dug down into the fiery sand until his hands bled. He had no
tools. Eventually he found water. It tasted harsh and bitter but he
drank and struggled on. Again and again as he toiled across the desert
he dug down with his bare hands to find water. Often it was bitter, but
he had to drink it just the same if he was to reach the better place.

At last he came to the end of the desert and found cool grass for his
feet, and shade for his head, and sweet water. As he rested he looked
back across the shimmering sand and saw another figure coming
towards him. He saw that this man was walking swiftly, where he had
crawled painfully, and was whistling cheerfully, where he had licked at
dry lips.

When the newcomer reached him, he asked, 'Have you crossed the
whole desert?'

'I have,' the stranger answered, 'and rapidly. Every time I felt thirsty
there was another spring of water, and between the springs there was a

pathway to follow. It was as if a pathway had been laid before me.'

This story is not a story of a remarkable person, who travelled from rags to riches through a series of dramatic adventures, disasters and triumphs. It is more ordinary than that. It is a story with hopes and desires, mistakes and misfortunes, successes and failures as there are in anyone's life.

I begin the story with the mistake that forced me to recognise that while I had been climbing the ladder of success it had been *leaning firmly up against the wrong wall.* That is a great metaphor I learned from Dr Stephen Covey who eventually became one of the many 'Masters' whose teaching transformed my life.

The discovery forced me, reluctantly at first, back to school. I had always been a poor performer at school, a lazy learner, but this time I had something real to learn and I had acquired some key pointers as to where to start learning it.

Over the past eight years I have read literally hundreds of books on the pursuit of human achievement and excellence; I have listened to thousands of hours of audiotapes by the gurus of business success and personal excellence; and I have looked at every measurement of achievement I could find, the financial laws, the corporate laws, even the spiritual laws of success.

At first, maybe like you, I found that every book I read, every audiotape I listened to, every culture I visited seemed to tell me different things. For a long time my principal reward was bewilderment and a growing frustration. Gradually, and almost imperceptibly, significant patterns and recurring themes emerged. I have found that it is not the things which teachers from many diverse generations and cultures say that are *different* from one another that are going to make the changes in everybody's lives. It is the things they say that are the *same.*

When I hear the same thing said today by business leaders in America that Socrates said in Europe, that the Vedic sages and the Buddhists said in Asia, that Christian and Muslim philosophers said all over the world, then I pay attention. When I notice that psychologists, physicists and poets are repeating the same phrases, again and again, I start to look for the inherent truths in what they say.

I believe that these truths are the *universal laws of human attainment and achievement,* consistent across all history and all peoples. It is the passing on of these truths that intrigues me. It is the task of playing my part in this that sometimes daunts me.

After I had read the first twenty-five books I thought that I knew everything there was to know about this field. Now, with every book I read, I realise that my journey has only just begun.

If in my book I can map out for you some of the territories I have explored and help you along *your* pathways, I will also be giving myself essential reminders of those same key issues. It is only on this basis that I have been able to square up to the conceit of writing such a book.

The incessant voice inside my head asking me who I thought I was, setting about such a task, was finally quietened when I read the introduction to Joseph Jaworski's life-changing book *Synchronicity – The Inner Path of Leadership.* In it he quotes the words of John of the Ladder, written in the seventh century: 'If some are still dominated by their former bad habits, and yet can teach by mere words, let them teach. For perhaps, by being put to shame by their own words, they will eventually begin to practise what they teach.'

I believe we teach best what we ourselves most need to know, and we write best about the lessons we most need to learn.

My map may not always lay out the precise route you want to follow, but if you have, as yet, no clearly defined map of your own it may give you a starting point and new pathways to explore. Even if you already have a map of your own, then sometimes it helps to confirm that for someone else there were also dragons, and that there is more than one way of slaying, or avoiding them; and sometimes that there may be other paths to explore, and other treasures to discover.

This, then, is the story – so far.

1: CRISIS

*When written in Chinese the
word crisis is composed of
two characters. One represents
danger and the other
represents opportunity.*

JOHN F. KENNEDY

*I*t had been the worst time of my life. And this was the
worst day: or so it seemed then. There was worse to come.
It was the day on which what I did was crazy, insane,
certifiable – but I did it. When I walked out of that room I
walked out of a job, out of a career, out of a life, and into –
what? Financial ruin was a certainty. I had nothing planned. I
had enormous debts, and now I had no way of paying them.
Yet, I walked out knowing that. I chose to do so.

Nearly five years of work had gone into the project, and I
was walking away from it. The Royal Britain Exhibition, a
heritage attraction telling the story of one thousand years of
our Royal history, had been my all-consuming passion for five
years of my life. It was brilliant in some respects and
catastrophic in others. In terms of its creativity, in terms of its
genius, in terms of the quality of what we had built it was
second to none. We had brought in craftsmen, artists,
designers and multi-media producers from different fields who
had never created a tourist attraction before. We had
completely redevised and redesigned how tourism and our
heritage could be interpreted. There was nothing else like it in
the United Kingdom. We were pioneers. We had cracked it.

We had turned an underground labyrinth into a walk

through one thousand years of history. As visitors passed the ticket office they stepped into the swirling mists of pre-history where ghostly images of ancient rulers appeared in an audio visual assault on the senses – King Alfred, Boudicca, and the invading Romans setting the scene for our island's story. Next the visitor came to the coronation of King Edgar, the first king of all England, and then set out on a procession through the betrayals, warrior deaths, murders, love stories, achievements and indiscretions of our 51 monarchs up to and including Queen Elizabeth II. We told the whole story through projection, moving holograms, mechanical theatres, sculptures and the wizardry of audiovisual technology – and not a waxwork in sight.

We had done a magnificent job, but we hadn't produced a populist exhibition, and we had badly miscalculated the marketing, so nobody knew we were there. Sixty per cent of the people who visited the attraction raved enthusiastically about what they saw. Forty per cent felt that it was too 'clever', and wasn't lively and bright enough; it wasn't fun.

The forty per cent were right – a lot had been compromised out of the budget. We had pared away so much of the flesh that only the skeleton remained; the 'clever' bits, the inventive bits, the cerebral bits. Those bits might have been brilliant, but what was missing was the excitement, the pageant, and the anecdotal storytelling that would bring the event to life.

There was no disagreement about that and there was plenty we could have done about it, but I believed the fundamental problem, what was going to cripple the business, was the fact that we had consistently mismanaged the marketing. We had raised £5 million from a private share issue; we had raised £200,000 from the English Tourist Board; we had opened on time; we had opened, more or less, on budget: and instead of there being 10,000 people knocking on the door to get in, there had been a handful. The caterers weren't at all happy.

They had prepared roast turkeys and roast lambs, smoked salmon and a thousand sandwiches, a high-quality buffet for a high-quality restaurant for a high-quality tourist attraction, and there was no one there to buy anything.

Our first visitor, the first guy in the queue, was from the USA. He had heard and read about it in the States. Our PR seemed to have been excellent on the other side of the Atlantic. As he came through the doors I decided that I wanted to treat our first visitor, so I bought him the first ticket. I still have the ticket – its net cost to me now incalculable. It is just about all I have to show for five years' work and an investment of £7 million. He went through, and came out as though he had been through a life-changing experience. Those first visitors on that first day went through the exhibition saying it was the most extraordinary thing they'd ever been through. We thought, 'Well, the numbers aren't what we thought they should be, but they like it – we've made it.'

The numbers didn't pick up. I was convinced that we could correct the weaknesses of the Exhibition, but without a radical rethink of the marketing we could not succeed. I failed to gain agreement from my colleagues on the Board. While I didn't disagree with them about the content of the Exhibition, they disagreed fundamentally with me about the strategy for pulling it around, getting the travel and tourist industry to take the project seriously, and getting the visitors through the doors. I believed we were going to repeat the same marketing mistakes we had made at the beginning. I would have been prepared to take risks and make different mistakes but I could not bring myself to repeat lessons which we should have learned. I couldn't have implemented a strategy that I knew in my heart was wrong.

It wasn't until years later that I realised the extraordinary power that is inherent in following your instincts, your gut feelings, rather than always pursuing a rational, logical path. If

I had known it at the time, it wouldn't have taken me two years to get back on my feet again. All I knew was that someone had to make a decision.

I made my decision. I met with the Board to agree the final rights issue document we had been putting together over the last few weeks. I told them that the document was not something I could sign. I also told them that it was more complicated than simply handing in my resignation. I had invested everything I owned in the company, not just emotionally, but financially.

In fact I had invested much more than I owned. I had borrowed a great deal to invest in my shares. I couldn't just walk away from that investment. I needed to know that they would listen to what I was saying was wrong with the business. I wanted their authority to implement a strategy that was utterly different from that which we had laid down in our offer to shareholders.

We needed to put ourselves in the shoes of the visitors. We needed to address our problems from the point of view of the travel trade companies on whom we depended. We should have been building professional relationships with the coach trade, hotels, and travel journalists. We should have been developing joint promotional deals with the railways and with other tourist attractions. We required simple, attractive and compelling posters, leaflets and radio campaigns to stir the imagination of our audience. We had become, more than once, victims of our own obsession with cleverness and intellectual pomposity. Our posters were visually and historically clever – and meaningless to our audience. Our radio campaign was the first ever two-minute radio commercial in the UK – and meaningless to listeners. We had largely ignored the key players in the industry who could determine our popularity and our fate. I knew that we would have to make radical changes to our business mentality if we were to stand any chance of turning the enterprise around. I was not convinced that we were the right people to do this.

A long, bloodless, but tense meeting took place. The long and short of it was that I walked away from the company. I had failed to persuade my partners of my fears or convince them of my solutions.

I met my wife, Francesca, back at my office at the exhibition site. We had been discussing for weeks how things were going, and what should happen. We took a last walk around the building. For the first time in my life *business* had brought me literally to tears. I remember standing there, unable to see clearly through the sadness. I couldn't believe that five years of my life had gone into this unfinished project.

> *Failure after long perseverance is much grander than*
> *never to have a striving good enough to be*
> *called a failure*
> GEORGE ELIOT

Not only were Francesca and I walking away from the building but we were walking into massive debt. I was walking away from my job, I was walking away from my only income and I was walking into a £250,000 debt that couldn't be serviced. I had hit the wall.

Within days, it seemed, Francesca announced that she was expecting our first child.

2: WILDERNESS

We are all of us failures – at least the best of us are.

SIR J. M. BARRIE

To start with there was a feeling of numbness. There weren't many tears now, and there wasn't much anger. I felt empty, floating above the scene unfolding at a distance from me. That chapter in my life seemed to be over, but there were still deep scars remaining. The financial scars were with me every day. The pain would take some months to surface.

For the first nine months, until my daughter Sophie was born, I busied myself by setting up an office, setting up a company, and chasing after half a hundred possible projects. I had decided that the one thing I had always wanted to do was to make television programmes. The idea came out of nowhere.

Within a week I had set up a company called Adrian Gilpin Television. I had no experience in this field, though Francesca worked in television as a production manager at that time, and we had a lot of colleagues in the television world. I had created theatre and tourism projects, now I could create television projects.

Over the period of those nine months I wrote 40 or 50 television proposals, sent off in a random way to every conceivable commissioning editor I could find. I joined all the television production associations. I went to all the meetings. I put my face around. Amazingly, I was approached by one or two established producers and set up working relationships for developing ideas.

We fired off ideas for mid-afternoon quiz show format programmes, documentaries, and even a major television marathon History of Europe; a modest collection of proposals for newcomers, designed to make their producers a great deal of money! Nothing came of any of them. I think we could have written *Hamlet*, but nothing would have come of it. Commissioning editors didn't want to have anything to do with us. We were upstarts without the money to develop our own product. We were outsiders, and their industry, like so many others, was enormously chauvinist.

I was able to find all sorts of reasons and justifications why people weren't doing business with me. What I didn't know at the time was that the real reason, the truth of it, was that these projects were being driven only by a desperate financial need. They were not being driven by my passion or by any sense of purpose other than to make fast money, to dig myself out of ever deepening debt. There was something missing from all those proposals. There was no heart or soul in them, no spark to make them happen. So, they didn't.

Nine months into this wilderness Sophie was born and, somehow, life seemed to settle. We had renegotiated interest terms; we had grown used to servicing the debt; we were just keeping going, jogging along. Sophie was born in May and I spent that beautiful, hot summer of 1989 working in the garden, with my newborn daughter beside me. It was an idyll.

Canker in the Apple

Nonetheless, there was a desperate restlessness inside. I built rockeries, planted borders and shrubberies, and decorated the house in what now seems a kind of manic defiance of the truth I knew deep inside me, that we were going to have to leave it.

Then that gut instinct, which I have since learned to understand and trust, told me that we had to get out of the house before other people started telling us we had to. Despite the fact that, for the time being anyway, our lenders were not being difficult I decided to take charge. Something inside me said, 'We're going to sell the house, we're going to sell the car: we're going to sell because we *choose* to. We're going to clear this debt.'

Bit by bit I began selling the assets we had, and paying off the mortgages. We moved into my grandmother's house to look after her. Seventeen months after Sophie, our second daughter, Phoebe, was born.

Still television projects continued to pour out to producers and production companies. We came very close with some of our projects, but by now I was beginning to feel that if there wasn't going to be short-term gain from television, there was no other reason for doing it. I had to find another way of earning a living. I had to exorcise the lingering ghosts of my failure to make the Exhibition succeed.

I still knew perfectly well that my own strategy for turning that business around would have been high-risk, and might not have worked. Even more decidedly I knew, as I had known then, that my colleagues' strategy would fail. Then, suddenly my worst predictions and nightmares came true. The company became insolvent and announced voluntary liquidation. I had been proved right in that, at least. Now everything had gone – not just my investment, but the project itself and the legacy of it. The doors had closed.

It wasn't until that moment that I realised that this chapter of my life had closed, too. I assumed it had closed when I walked away from the company, but psychologically I had only put the baby into intensive care when I walked away. Now the baby was dead and gone for ever.

It was at about this time that I visited a leading career psychologist. I knew that I didn't belong to the television culture, and was increasingly questioning whether I had any real desire to make television programmes at all. On the other hand, I wasn't earning and I wasn't going to be able to recreate the job that had collapsed around me. No one, I thought, was going to be interested in the services of someone who had run a multi-million-pound business that had disappeared without trace.

Maybe it was me? Nothing I was doing was working. Why me? Why was it that everything I touched went sour? Was I ever going to find anything that really stimulated me?

So I sat down with my vocational psychologist. I went through an entire day of executive psychometric profiling, which didn't teach me a great deal. There were no revelations on that day, only a focusing on the hard truth that ex-entrepreneurs are hard to employ. Once you have tasted the bitter-sweet freedom of running your own business, you are uncomfortable company for senior teams in a professional business.

Those who cannot tell what they desire, or expect,
still sigh and struggle with indefinite thoughts
and with vast wishes.
RALPH WALDO EMERSON

Though I didn't know it at the time, the seeds of one of the most powerful revelations of all were planted with what the psychologist said next.

'Adrian, if your psychometric tests had revealed incipient schizophrenia no one could have been surprised. Your whole career darts about from place to place, activity to activity. It seems to lack any sense of direction or purpose. Adrian, what do you want?'

I didn't know; I hadn't a clue. I was so caught up in the frenzied energy of activity trying to dig my way out of my financial mess, working sixteen hours a day in the belief that the harder you worked the more likely you were to succeed, that I had never paused to think about something so apparently simple.

I don't think she expected me to give her an answer there and then. I didn't, but for weeks and weeks after that meeting her words were lodged in my subconscious, nagging away at me. It was months before I began to realise the power of that simple question:

'Adrian, *what do you want?*'

I went home feeling that I hadn't learned anything that was going to make a difference, only that I was on my own. Even when that potent question resurfaced from time to time I still didn't know the answer. I never *had* known the answer. The only thing I could ever remember wanting was to be an actor. After a number of years in the theatre industry I had realised that even that wasn't what I really wanted. It wasn't enough so, inevitably, it was the reason that I wasn't good enough to excel.

I could not remember ever wanting to go to school, or even being able to tell anyone what I wanted for Christmas or my birthday. People would ask me what I wanted, and I would say, 'I don't know'. They would make a few suggestions and I would say, 'No, I don't want that, I don't want that.' Like many people, I just didn't know. So, there at least was a point from which I could begin. I could start by identifying some of the things I *didn't* want.

I didn't want to be an actor any more. I didn't even want to become the world's greatest television producer. I didn't want to be an administrator, or a manager of other people's ideas. I didn't want to be a management consultant, advising other businesses how to do their strategic planning or their marketing planning, where I wouldn't be engaged, or involved. I didn't want to be alone. I didn't want to be living in a cramped house. I didn't want us to be living with my grandmother. I didn't want to be doing nothing. There were all sorts of things I *didn't* want.

I didn't know how to discover what I did want. I simply felt that there was a need for some positive thoughts to replace negative ones. I began to take stock of what I had. First and foremost, I had a wonderful wife, and two adorable children, seventeen months apart. I had been at home with these children. I had watched them come into this world. I had been watching them grow. I had been at home with Francesca through all that period which most fathers miss, and it had been wonderful. I didn't want to miss any of it in the future.

With that first inkling of something I wanted to keep, my thinking began almost imperceptibly to shift. I knew that I didn't want to be working so damned hard that I never saw my children grow. I didn't want to be going back to what I had been doing before the Exhibition, putting on theatre shows all around the country and the world – pantomimes in Tel Aviv, Canada, Sydney, London, Manchester and a hundred other less exciting places. I didn't want those things because I *did* want to watch my children grow up. I wanted to do things that most men don't get a chance to do.

It was a sudden and unexpected chink of light in the black mist that had been surrounding me. There was something about watching children grow and develop that started making me think that what I would really like to be doing was nurturing not just children but people. What would make me feel really good would be to have the skills to start making other people feel good about themselves, about their jobs and about what they wanted. I had no idea how this might happen, I just knew it seemed to be something that I actually wanted.

While I was thinking about this with a new energy and optimism, I came across the answer Thomas Edison gave when he was asked how he had kept going through hundreds of failed experiments in his search for the first practical incandescent light bulb. He said that he had never *had* a failed experiment. Every experiment had produced a result. It may not have been the result he wanted, it may not have been the one he expected, but it was a result he could learn from. With the amount of information that was available to him after hundreds and hundreds of different results how could he possibly fail?

I thought, 'Of course, with the amount of information I have got about what makes a tourist attraction collapse, I can go on to help other people to make damned sure they don't do the same thing.' Edison had taught me that I had not failed, I had just had a different result from the one I had expected. This 'failure' contained precious jewels of experience, opportunities to learn something of immense value. Crucially, I knew how and why we had failed. With all my experience about how *not* to build a tourist attraction I had a product to sell!

> *I'd much rather climb into the head of someone who has lost and see what made that person come back to be a victor, than to climb into the head of a winner.*
> RAFER JOHNSON (DECATHLON OLYMPIC GOLD MEDAL 1960)

I didn't know it, but that was the beginning, just the beginning, of the turnaround. There were still unwanted, apparent failures, and unexpected events to come.

3: WANDERINGS

l am not discouraged, because every wrong attempt
discarded is another step forward.

THOMAS EDISON

Within days of making that decision to use my recent experiences, to use what I had once seen as my failure as a stepping stone, another experience came out of the blue. It was to have a major impact on me.

Suddenly I received a phone call from a colleague who had participated in the Exhibition project, asking if I would help a consortium develop a proposal to create and manage a massive European Rivers Festival. They knew about the Exhibition and its demise. They said, 'You've obviously got some good experience of what to avoid. Would you like to come and talk with us?'

To create the festival we needed resources: we needed a team. We started looking for backers and names to give the project credibility. My colleagues had an open door to a good 'name' for the letterhead and the investment brochure: a member of the House of Lords. I met him, and he agreed to consider giving his support and endorsement to the project. He was to be our 'Lord on the Board'.

In the end the project never happened It was not developed enough, there wasn't the money, and we were going to have to raise our own finance for it. I decided it wasn't right for us. A month or so ago I would have thought, 'another failure'.

But, from the instant I had decided to use my 'failures' as stepping stones, my whole psychology, my outlook, my map of the world had changed. Far from failing, I had made a new link. New connections had started. They might lead everywhere, they might lead nowhere, but they had started.

Our new aristocratic contact owned an historic manor house, open for part of each year as a tourist attraction. When we were discussing his possible rôle on the advisory committee for the Rivers Festival project I quietly made a trip down to have a look. I had visited the house and its gardens as a child. It was fascinating to wander around now with my professional, if slightly dented, experience of tourism management. A few moments after I walked into the house I felt the most extraordinary feeling in the pit of my stomach.

The smell of untapped potential, of missed opportunity, of uninspired management was palpable. In every corner lurked the signals of the half-hearted commercialism mastered by the owners and managers of our architectural heritage. They were the tell-tale signs of reluctant exploitation; the embarrassed cocktail of a need to earn money with a deeply ingrained dislike and mistrust of commercialism. I realised, with a sense of certainty, that here was something I could do: I realised that a sequence of events had brought me to this place for a reason. This was where I could put my knowledge and experiences to work; where I could lay the Exhibition ghosts once and for all.

I said to Francesca, 'I could transform this business.' It was instinctive, a gut feeling again.

I engineered a meeting with the owner and his advisers. Within a month I had been asked to join him to help to turn his business around. He, too, was keen to shed the style of an older generation and face the future with a new, high-quality approach.

Working with some of the theories I had believed were right for the Exhibition, and with some of the new theories I was beginning to develop about businesses and about management, we became, within twelve months, the fastest-growing heritage business in the UK. We turned a six-figure loss into a six-figure profit and we won an award for marketing – the very factor that had scuppered the Royal Britain Exhibition!

I had negotiated a contract which paid me a comparatively small retainer, but gave me a fair share of the commercial success of the venture. Income was beginning to flow, and with the increasing success of the business I was continuing to clear my remaining debts.

Francesca and I lived very frugally. We moved out of my grandmother's house into a tiny cottage in the Kent country-side. We produced a son, Charlie, determined to keep building the family that was so important to us. The time I needed to invest in this project was considerable if I was to achieve the results I believed were possible. Our cottage was less than three hundred yards from my office; time with my young family became all the more precious as I set about rebuilding a life that I would be happy to live. After our first year in the job, we moved to a larger farmhouse and brought our own furniture out of storage. We were beginning to take charge again.

I was working on a project that was not going to make me a fortune, but was going to make me considerably more than a salary. The work we were doing was sufficiently successful for my client and his colleagues to suggest that we set up a joint tourism consultancy, to transfer our joint lessons and experiences of the last couple of years down through the industry.

It seemed a sensible, logical move. We had become a high profile success and there was clearly an opportunity to market our experiences and our skills. It was a time for optimism, energy and high excitement. That wasn't what happened.

With a dawning horror I realised that I had been sucked into something for which I had no real interest or passion. It wasn't me: it wasn't what I wanted. I began watching myself get up in the morning, watching myself go to work, watching myself pull together strategies and business plans for people and for businesses that I wasn't excited by. I was being reasonably successful but somewhere there was an unsettling feeling that somehow, despite the success, it was not what I wanted. Dr Stephen Covey's words started to ring in my ear: I was climbing back up the ladder of success, but I *still* had my ladder set firmly up against the wrong wall.

Again, there came a chink of light. I had begun discussions with the Kent Training and Enterprise Council (Kent TEC) about making our consultancy company different. Training and Enterprise Councils are regional bodies throughout the UK, largely funded by government grant, to administer statutory training programmes and promote awareness of the value of developing professional and personal skills in the workforce. Each TEC decides its own specific agenda and Kent TEC was beginning to demonstrate an unusual degree of innovation in its approach to learning.

I wanted to enhance the consultancy process with the findings from my studies into how people and businesses become successful. If, out of our experiences and my studies, we could begin to teach people in the industry how to find their own solutions by thinking strategically, we could eliminate the need for them to call upon expensive and time-consuming consultancy every time problems arose. By coaching them to think differently, their problems might never become problems at all. Kent TEC liked the concept and, while they had not yet agreed anything, wanted to take it further.

Then one of those chance moments, which we often call coincidences, threw everything I was doing into a different light. Later I understood that it was not a matter of co-incidence; just that while my conscious mind was busily engaged upon the prospect of escape from the financial snares, my subconscious mind was still ruminating upon my career psychologist's powerful question.

4: THE CINDER PATH

Come to the edge
no we'll fall

Come to the edge
no we can't

Come to the edge
no we're afraid

and they came

and he pushed them

and they flew

GUILLAUME APOLLINAIRE

While we were still setting up the new consultancy, a mailing sheet arrived on my desk, advertising the American business guru Anthony Robbins, leading an event in Birmingham. I put it in the bin. I never went to those sorts of seminars. I religiously ignored any mail-outs from the American-influenced personal development gurus. Any time I received a 'Change Your Life In Thirty Seconds', 'The Easy Way To Riches', 'A Thousand Ways To Make Yourself A Millionaire Overnight', 'Discover Your Innermost Power' – anything like that would go straight in the bin. I assumed they were all thinly disguised sales platforms for multi-level businesses or pyramid investment schemes. I had read Dale Carnegie and similar writers, but I had no idea that there was a massive industry of motivational speakers bouncing up and down on stages from the East to the West coast of America. I had never heard of Anthony Robbins but this time, even though I had put the leaflet in the bin, just as usual, for some reason it had registered in my memory and it was lingering there.

One evening, three or four months later, I was at home. It was a Monday. Francesca buys the *Guardian* newspaper on a Monday, and it was lying open on the table. There was an article about Anthony Robbins coming to Birmingham – his first ever visit to the UK. It was the sort of article that, normally, I would have completely ignored. For some reason I stopped to read it. The message was very Californian, and seemed very materialistic, highly unrealistic and unlikely to attract much interest on this side of the Atlantic. Usually I would have forgotten it almost immediately but again, for some reason, a thought nagged at me all evening. The article had said that Robbins was coming to Birmingham that week. I said to Francesca, 'You know, I think I might like to go and see this.'

For twenty-four hours the ideas in the article pervaded my thoughts. I found myself looking at my diary wondering if I could make sufficient changes to get myself up to Birmingham for Friday evening. Eventually I rang the office of the company promoting the event. The tickets were £500. There was no justification for me to charge the cost to the business. I was still seriously in debt, so I had to forget it.

But I couldn't. On the Thursday I made a phone call to the Kent TEC. I said, 'There's some interesting work being done in the States, and there's an American coming over whom I think we should be paying attention to. It might impact the learning and development work that we're doing with companies and individuals over here. Would you sponsor me to go and see whether it's something we should be taking seriously in Kent?'

The answer came back within the hour: 'Look, I can only give you £250 towards it without having to go to any further authority. Obviously, there isn't time for that.'

I said, 'That'll do. I'll pay the rest myself.'

I phoned the promoting company, asking if there were any tickets left. There was no one there who could answer my question – they were all up in Birmingham!

That did it. I said to Francesca, 'I'm sorry, but I'm going away for the weekend.' I packed a suitcase and I drove to Birmingham without a ticket. This was becoming an adventure. I couldn't explain the sudden emotional need I had to be at this event. It was as if something was guiding my hand, leading me there. I arrived at the reception desk in the National Exhibition Centre. There seemed to be hundreds of people milling around. Still being prompted by an unfamiliar voice in my head, I said very cheekily, 'I am here representing the Training and Enterprise Council in Kent. It's a non-profit-making organisation. We're very interested in Mr Robbins' work but we have very limited budgets and can't afford £500. Are there any last-minute discounts?'

The girl at the desk said, 'The man to ask is standing right there', and pointed to the promoter. He looked at me: 'I don't know – how about £250?' The exact amount I had in sponsorship.

An hour or so later, I walked into the hall. Pop music was blasting out from all corners. There were dancers on the stage and participants leaping around on the chairs. I thought, 'I've come to some sort of Southern Baptist Revival meeting. What on earth am I doing?' From the looks on some of the faces at the back with me there were other Britons asking themselves a similar question. A large Dutch contingent was taking careful note of the nearest exits.

'Well,' I thought, 'I'm here now. I've booked into the hotel. I might as well stay and see what's going on.'

Half an hour later, on to the stage came the great man, six-foot-seven of him and with an even larger Californian personality. Within a few minutes he had impressed his audience as an extraordinarily powerful communicator. Then he asked

19

the question, 'How many of you are here for the fire walk?' Out of the 1200 people there 1,199 put their hands up. I looked around and thought, 'What fire walk?' I remembered vaguely that an hour or so earlier in the maelstrom that was the NEC I had signed a piece of paper that said something about releasing my rights in respect of the fire walk. I had presumed it was some sort of publicity stunt and thought no more about it. My naïveté was staggering.

Now it was gradually dawning on me that at some point later in the evening I, and 1,199 other people, were going to be asked to walk across twelve feet of burning coal. Were we all going to become completely insane? Had we become involved in some cult?

The man had enormous credibility and enormous power. I hung around to see if I would walk across the coals with everybody else, and, if I lived to tell the tale, what sort of experience it would be.

So, I went through the evening. At about midnight we were all ushered outside where we watched Robbins light a number of log fires. We watched as the flames flickered and grew until they had exploded into frantic tongues of orange heat. Robbins' voice, powerful and hypnotic, coaxed us all into taking our turn to come close to the fires and feel the heat. He told us that in two or three hours the coals would have reached temperatures high enough to melt steel and that we would be breaking through our terror and stepping out and walking across them.

For the next few hours we listened to stories of ordinary people deciding to do extraordinary things. We were coached in the technique of fire-walking. We learned how to take complete command of our state of mind. We learned a (refreshingly appropriate) mantra to repeat in our heads as we crossed the coals: 'Cool moss, cool moss, cool moss'. We were reminded that stopping in fear halfway across would not be comfortable. We were taught how to celebrate our victorious crossing with a passionate physical and vocal exclamation of joy. The British audience was moving perceptibly out of its comfort zone, and was starting to enjoy it. This giant Californian may be insane, but he is convincing and fun. The Brits were playing full out and inhibitions were evaporating into the air.

At about two o'clock in the morning I, the even more mystified Dutchmen and 1,100 highly over-excited people were asked to take our shoes and socks off. We walked barefoot into the cold October night in Birmingham. There was a soft drizzle making the ground even colder and damp. We formed queues and listened to Tony explain the rules. A small group of musicians started to beat out a penetrating rhythm on African drums. The lines of people moved slowly. My feet became so wet I thought even the heat of melted steel would not penetrate the cold I felt. My heart was beating, partly in time to the drums and partly through the mix of fear and excitement that every person there was feeling. 'More coals, more coals!' Robbins would cry, and a wheelbarrow full of hot coals would be guided past us by the fire-builders. Shovels would scoop up the white-hot embers and scatter them in a crust on the ground in front of the waiting adventurers.

As I approached the front of my line, I gathered every atom of self-control I could muster, I recalled the last two hours of coaching. I repeated the mantra, 'Cool moss, cool moss'. I was next. 'Get into state,' commanded the line captain. 'You are ready, go!'

Six steps into madness and then the explosion of bliss as I felt the icy water from the hose-pipe drench my feet and legs. 'Wipe your feet and celebrate!' came the command, too late, as I was jumping with joy like a child, hugging just about anyone I bumped into. My feet felt as though they were on fire and yet there was no pain, no blisters, no marks, no scars to carry away from this journey through fear.

At 3am, back in the hotel I rang Francesca. 'Darling, did I wake you? I've just done a fire walk.'

'Very nice, darling,' she said, 'do you know what time it is?'

'No, no, listen: I've walked barefoot across twelve feet of burning coals.'

'What? Really? I thought you meant it as some sort of metaphor. Really? You've really walked across . . .?' She was wide awake by now, telling me to come home, and '*Don't sign anything*!'

It had been a bizarre experience for most of the audience; it would have been a bizarre experience for most people outside California; but it was a very powerful one. During the weekend it became evident to me that whatever it was that had driven me there, the unsettled feelings that I had about the consultancy, about tourism, were muddled and confused. During those two and a half very wacky, very Californian days I realised that I needed to sort out what I was all about.

Robbins had asked that same question again, 'What do you really want?' Then came the most powerful and frightening question of all, 'If you knew that you could not possibly fail . . . what would you do for the rest of your life?'

I had no answer. Once again, I didn't know. Not knowing was a terrible feeling.

I had been back on a career path for some time now but it was only at that moment that I realised that I didn't know where the path was taking me – didn't know where I *wanted* it to take me. I really had no idea what I wanted to be.

5: A NEW ROAD

You will never succeed while smarting under the
drudgery of your occupation, if you are constantly
haunted with the idea that you could succeed better in
something else.

ORISON SWETT MARDEN

At the end of the Birmingham event we were given the
opportunity, in the true American style that I have
come to love, to buy the product they were *really* trying
to sell us – not a £500 conference but a £5500 seminar which,
with travel and hotels in the States, would cost me in excess of
£12,000. Despite what Francesca had said, I signed up for it
before I even left the room, knowing that I was about to go
home and say, 'Darling, you know we're still £40,000 in debt?
Well, we're now going to be £50,000 in debt.'

I signed up in the back of the room because I knew that if I
went home to think about committing myself to a £12,000
training programme, and if I put together a plan in the
traditional way of 'Where am I going to raise the money, how
am I going to do this?', it would become one more project that
choked in the planning weeds, and died. Having made the
psychological and financial commitment in the back of the
conference hall, I now had no choice. I had to find a way.

I had spent two and half days listening to this man talk about
the extraordinary flow that only starts when you become fully
committed. I wanted to test it. I was saying, 'OK, show me; show
me how.'

Not 'how', but 'why'?

We learned many major lessons during that weekend. One was that you do not need to know *how* to do something before you start. You need to know *why* you want to do it before you start. One of the driving forces behind human achievement is not knowing how to do something, but knowing what you want, and knowing why. Almost anything of excellence that human beings have achieved, they have achieved where there wasn't a 'how' to know. When people first invented a new technology, or laid railways, or drove a tunnel through a mountain, or flew to the moon, there were no 'how to's. Edison didn't know how to make the light bulb. Steven Spielberg didn't know how he was going to get to direct his first movie. Gandhi didn't know how he would free India from British rule. Nelson Mandela didn't know how to rid his nation of apartheid, or even if it was possible in his lifetime. All these people could do at first was imagine it. There never are any 'how to's if you're doing something that no one has ever done before.

This is not only true if you are a human being trying to do something that humanity has never done before; it is equally true of you as a person, thinking about something that you, individually, haven't done before. It may be that you can read a book on 'how to', but you, personally, still don't know how *you* are going to do whatever it is you are starting.

Standing at the back of that room in Birmingham I didn't know how I was going to raise the money. I had been listening for two and a half days to a man telling me I didn't need to know how, I only needed to know why. I knew precisely why. I wanted, on three occasions over the next twelve months, to surround myself with twelve hundred people who were utterly committed to becoming their best. I wanted to absorb the teaching, read the books, but most of all to spend time with people who knew how to discover what they want, and how to go and get it. I could just have read the books and listened to the tapes – everything that Robbins teaches is available in a book, everything he teaches is available on a tape – but for me, there was more to it than that.

I wanted to be around people who were committed to excellence, to listen to some of the best people in their fields. We were going to listen to Norman Schwarzkopf; we were going to listen to some of the world's most successful investors in the stock markets; we were going to listen to Jim Hansberger, Senior Vice President of Shearson Lehman Brothers/ American Express and one of America's most successful investment strategists; to Peter Lynch who took the Fidelity Magellan Fund from \$20 million to \$14 billion making it the largest investment fund in the world; and to Sir John Templeton, one of the most innovative and successful investors in history. We were going to hear some of the leading authorities on Mind/Body Healing, people like Deepak Chopra whose books and lecture tours have become legendary in America, England and India; we were going to hear some of the leading authorities on relationship-management, people like John Gray, author of the international bestseller *Men Are from Mars, Women Are from Venus.*

We were going to listen to the life stories of immigrant millionaires like Lee Van Vu, who arrived in a strange country with not a currency note in his pockets, with not even the language of the country he was entering. He was eleven years old in 1954 when his wealthy family were expelled from Hanoi to South Vietnam. He trained as a lawyer. He was later tortured and imprisoned for his 'dissident' political views. For the second time in his life he became a refugee, when Saigon fell in 1976. He escaped in a small boat and made the long journey to Guam, then to Denver and finally to work as a cleaner in a bakery in Houston. He is now a Texan tycoon with six successful businesses and an enormous wealth – financial and spiritual. We were going to discover from people like Lee Van

Vu, not *what* they did, not *how* they did it, but what mental paradigms, what attitudes and beliefs they needed to be successful. We were going to discover *why* they did what they did.

We were going to hear from people who had faced setbacks and challenges that I could only describe in the language of nightmares – mental and physical abuse at the hands of unresourceful people or the random tragedies of fate.

If these people could transcend the scale of their experiences, the occasional stumbles on *my* life's pathway came sharply into context. How could I not go to meet them?

The faculty on this programme would be extraordinary, exceptional people, legendary in their own fields, and we were going to listen to them all. That was why I wanted to go. I was beginning to gain a sense of what I wanted out of it, even if I didn't yet know what I wanted to do with the rest of my life.

I hadn't a clue how it was going to happen. According to the teaching you don't have to know how before you start. The process of starting tunes your psychology to finding the how. The how invariably comes *last*.

For all of my career up to this point I had been planning businesses, not only for myself but for other people, based on the nuts and bolts of 'how to'. My colleagues and I had started with the business plan; we had started with the financial forecasts, which almost invariably started with an analysis of the *costs* of the dream; we had gone step by step, 'Whom are we going to employ? What are they going to do?' Out of that we would build up the vision of where we wanted to go.

Every other successful business started the other way round. It started with the vision first: '*What* do we want to achieve? *Why* do we want to achieve it? Hell's teeth, nobody's ever done this before, so none of us have a clue how we are going to do it, so we'll find out as we go.' I already knew the what and the why. I was now going to go home to find out how to do this, to find out how to raise the money I needed to go to these seminars.

The second piece of teaching I wanted to test was that when you know why you want something, and you have started to take action, resources suddenly become available to you. I didn't need Robbins to teach me that whatever I wanted to do I needed people to assist me. I knew that *people* were the keys to unlock the resources I needed; I knew I had to be able to communicate my dream in a way that attracted not just the attention but the willing support and the active participation of other people.

The Magic of Rapport

You can, the conference told us, deliberately create rapport with the people around you. Subconsciously you already know the triggers: you automatically flick the switches of rapport when you are with people you like, people you find it easy to be with. When you are out of rapport with people something happens that is different. This silent mechanism is the key to influence, persuasion and powerful communication. It is perfectly possible to learn how to flick the switches of rapport whenever you want them, deliberately, consciously. You can learn how to put yourself in command of the process.

> *I do not believe in a fate that falls on men, however*
> *they act: but I do believe in a fate that falls on them*
> *unless they act.*
>
> G. K. CHESTERTON

I went home to test these propositions. I told Francesca that I had signed up for the seminars.

She looked at me. Without a moment's hesitation she said, 'I know. That's fine. I know that you'll find the money.' That total trust in my judgement, despite the fact that there was overwhelming evidence of its frailty, and despite the fact that I had just run us into the ground: that total certainty that if I set my mind to something it would happen, gave me an enormously powerful springboard from which to take the first leap of faith.

I made three phone calls. The first was to the Principal of a local college of further education, with whom I had had a little bit of contact. I said, 'You know about education, you know about learning: I want to go and explore some very innovative learning techniques that are being developed in America. Would this be something that you would be interested in sponsoring – not out of sheer goodwill, but in return for something I could do for you when I get back? I could brief you, or some of your staff. I could put together some seminars for your senior lecturers about these developments and techniques, about some of the radically new work that is being done in America on facilitating learning and on enabling people to achieve far beyond their current expectations. I think that might be useful to a further education college.'

He agreed. He couldn't put up £10,000 or £12,000, but he could put up £2,000 or £3,000. He would speak to the appropriate people and he would get things moving.

The second phone call I made was to the Kent TEC, who had provided the original £250 for me to attend the Birmingham conference. I said, 'There are some interesting ideas here. I'm about to fax you the report you've paid for. If we're really going to make this of value to us in Kent, and if we're going to be able to bring some of these ideas into the UK, we're going to need to find ways of translating them culturally. I need to go on the full programme and find out what's happening in California. You can bet your bottom dollar that it's going to be pretty wacky, but it's certainly going to be at the cutting edge of learning and development in any field. So let's investigate it. When I come back we'll run a series of pro-grammes over here.'

They said, 'OK, we like the idea. We can't invest £12,000, but we can invest £7,000 or £8,000.'

The third call was to the Chief Executive of the South East England Tourist Board, a professional association representing the interests of tourist businesses. I said, 'You know about my background in tourism, you know about my successes in tourism. Our work is predominantly in tourism at the moment. Do you have access to any development grants that could enable me to go and investigate some of the more dramatic things that are being done to develop people's thinking, including business thinking, in the States?'

He said, 'We like what you are doing: we would love to be able to help, but we have no remit to do that, and we have no discretionary budget available to do that. We're sorry, the answer is no.'

When they finally came back with their answers the college said I could have £2,500, and Kent TEC said I could have £7,500. Two successful calls out of three had provided me with ten of the twelve thousand I needed. I now had the money to pay for my tuition up front, and the greater part of the money to cover my flights and accommodation for the three-semester programme 'Mastery University'.

I was determined that this trip was not going to cost my new company or my new consultancy partners anything at all, until we knew for certain that there was something of substance for us in the long run. These two local organisations were pre-pared to back me privately and I would fund the balance myself. If the plan was successful I would be perfectly placed to position our consultancy at the forefront of this work in the UK. I believed my partners would be thrilled.

When I returned from the first module there was a friendly phone call from the Chief Executive of the South East England

Tourist Board to ask how the trip went. Then he said, 'I'd like you to come and get together with my Chairman. We are aware of what you are doing, and we are aware of your skills in tourism. We are also aware that you are looking at some very interesting work, and we would like you to help us to redevise our strategic business plan.'

I had made the decision to go, knowing the why, if not the how. Two phone calls out of three had established positive rapport, and positive support. The third call, which I might earlier have thought a failure, had had its own result, different from what I had wanted, and different from what I had expected. Instead of the financial grant to help me on my way before I went, within hours of my return my partners and I were being offered a £20,000 consultancy contract.

Two strands of my new thinking and my new learning were weaving together.

6: BLIND ALLEY

Fine timber does not grow with ease,
The stronger the wind, the stronger the trees.

ANON.

I returned from the first module in the States, in-
vigorated, and utterly inspired by the teaching, by the
stories of extraordinary achievers and thinkers, by
futurists talking about how the world may be in 50 or a 100
years' time, and by people who had encountered extraordinary
challenges in their lives. At the heart of it all were people whose
success seemed entirely dependent on their ability to think
through any circumstance that affected them and say, 'This
challenge could mean this, and it could mean that – *which
meaning serves me best?*'

I heard people describe bankruptcy, illness, disablement as
opportunities to start again, do new things, live better lives. I
listened to the stories of entrepreneurs who had made and
lost many millions, and at every setback they had stood up,
brushed themselves down and started all over again. None of
them described these events as I would have done –
'nightmare, disaster, collapse, horror'. They used words like
'challenge, opportunity, situation, chance to take a breath'.
Because they were describing the world differently from most
people they were experiencing it differently. We were all
consistently reminded of Henry Ford's words: 'Failure is only
the opportunity to more intelligently begin again.'

Yet, beneath the excitement, some of the restlessness and
dissatisfaction remained. Yes, *they* had risen to their challenges,
had seen the way ahead. Why hadn't I? Why not me?

31

I had always been able to think in that way for other people. A considerable number of them had profited from my hard work and my ideas, but none of it ever manifested itself in fulfilment, or appropriate reward for me. Yet again, here I was building up a consultancy business for myself and two partners because I had been so successful running my partner's historic house. Within weeks of setting up the consultancy we had landed one of the most prestigious projects in tourism: within weeks we had entered into negotiation with the Training and Enterprise Council about massive research funding for peak performance teams, and for training people to think in a new way.

I owned 49 per cent of the company and had no control: I owned 49 per cent of the company and I was on a fixed salary. Again I could see myself heading towards being successful and finding solutions for other people – but not for myself. The pattern was about to repeat itself: but to repeat itself for the last time.

On my return from California we started the project with the South East England Tourist Board. They started to pay us very well for it. I was roped on to all sorts of industry committees and boards, and I began building a high profile for our consultancy business in exactly the same way I had for my partner's historic house. We were being taken seriously. We were being asked to bid for some substantial projects.

In the late summer of that year I was on the final leg of the American programme. While I was in Hawaii, where the final semester was being held, I started to receive messages from my assistant at home that there was something wrong, that my partners were unhappy. They had started taking inappropriate executive decisions without me and I needed to get back as quickly as I could.

When I did get back all I found was a letter that set out only too clearly the fact that, happy as they were with the successes we had had in the first few months of the consultancy business, my partners felt that my plans were now diverging from their original concept. They wanted to sell their part of the consultancy, and sell it straight away. The tone of the letter was harsh and the message unambiguous. They wanted me to buy them out – as always intended – but, instead of buying them out gradually over several years, they wanted it to happen now.

I said, 'No.'

The track record of the company, so far, was good work for three clients – all of whom were personal contacts of mine before we started. I had put in my time, my partners had put in their money; we had both done what we said we would.

I told them that I would, indeed, buy them out because that was the original agreement, but over the five-year period we had agreed. Bit by bit as we hit certain targets I would buy more of the company back. It took several communications between fax machines to resolve the question. In our final dialogue they asked me, 'How certain are you about the contract with the TEC?'

'As certain as anyone can be. They are extremely interested, they have the money, they like what I'm doing. They have already supported me privately. I think we'll get it, but I don't know whether it will be six weeks or six months.'

That wasn't enough. They had decided that my desire to develop people's thinking and their desire to provide traditional consultancy were diverging too far.

Sir Leslie Porter, past Chairman of the Tesco supermarket chain, once said to me, 'Adrian, you know what a consultant is. He is someone who borrows your watch to tell you the time, then pockets the watch.' As a consultant I put plans together for a company – largely based on their own advice – added my own spin based upon my map of what *I* would do if I was them, and sent them a bill. I felt that Leslie's model was rather too close to the truth. I imposed my model, and left implementation, for better or worse, up to them.

Now I was much more interested in teaching people how to find their own solutions. Traditional consultancy often creates dependence. Once you have a client's trust they can reach the point where they can't move without you. My model was to guide people on to their own pathways, open the door for them and push them forward.

In the end, sadly, I refused to buy the business on my partners' terms. They wrote their investment off and withdrew. The consultancy closed down.

7: SATORI

However, there is a simple alternative that can be put into practice in a moment of satori, or instant awakening. You can drop your personal history right now. Just drop it.

DR WAYNE DYER

I was on my own again. I was extremely excited about it, but not a little rattled that, once again, the success that I was beginning to generate was being undermined by other people.

In a moment of deep frustration I ran the 'Why me?' routine to Francesca. 'Take the Royal Britain Exhibition. I put in all the work, but I was the only one who went bankrupt. The others may have lost a lot of money, but they could afford it. None of them had to cancel their summer holiday, let alone sell their house. And what have I achieved so far in my life? I've walked across burning coals, and what have I done with the rest of my life? I've managed to screw up a business. I've failed to provide properly for my family for the last few years. My projects all come to a sticky end. I've been doing a dead-end job that doesn't excite me . . .' and I reeled off a list of the failures that I had had all the way through my working career, ending with the demise of the tourism consultancy. I was feeling extremely sorry for myself.

Francesca looked at me, with a tear in her eye, and shook her head. 'That's simply not the way I see you. I don't recognise this person you're describing. With the Royal Britain Exhibition I see you as having had the greatest courage, because you were the only one who put his house on the line.

I see you as the only one who learned anything from the experience. Others are more than capable of making the same mistake again, but you won't. I saw you walk away from a project that meant almost as much to you as your family, because to stay would have been against your innermost instincts, and your innermost principles; whereas the others were prepared to stay with it, despite the fact that they didn't believe in it. I have never seen you as a victim. I have never seen you as someone who is constantly on the rough end of other people's decisions. You left the Exhibition because you chose to. You recognised that television production was the wrong industry for you. You decided to take charge of the debt long before the banks got nervous. You decided the Festival would not work and you were right. You decided the fate of the consultancy. You have always had the courage and integrity to do what you believe is right.'

As I listened to her describe the circumstances of my early business life, my theatre career, my time at the tourist attraction, my flirtation with television, my experiences at the historic house and with the consultancy it sounded to me like somebody else's life. We had been observing the same events, so how was it that our perceptions were so utterly different?

For the first time in my life, I consciously stopped for a moment and thought, 'This is really curious. Here we are both looking back at the same experiences. All of those things actually happened. But I have a completely different version of it. Francesca has seen a different story. We don't recognise each other's description of the world. Is it possible that there is no truth, except the one you choose to *believe*? Maybe to define those events in terms of absolute truth is just not possible. You can describe the same circumstances chronologically, put numbers and dates against them, but they only have meaning when you interpret them. After the Exhibition I was saying to myself, that means that I will never do anything again, that means that I am a failure, that means that nobody is going to back me. Francesca was saying, that means that you are courageous, that means that you will learn.'

Those maps couldn't have been further apart: the same dates, the same sequences, the same events. In that moment I realised that Francesca would now be making different decisions from me. If Anita Roddick or Richard Branson, Mother Teresa or Mahatma Gandhi had been through similar experiences, each of them would have decided to do something different. For each of them the realities would have been different.

It occurred to me then that it was just like Francesca with a crew making a movie for television. They would film a scene from a wide angle, then shoot the close-ups and reverse shots, then track the whole scene with a camera raised high on a crane. Then they would all go back to the editing suite and decide how they wanted the scene to look. During editing they could fundamentally change the whole meaning of the scene, depending on which angle they chose, and which sequence they put after which. It seemed no different from us as human beings. We do exactly the same thing.

I remembered the old television advertisement for the *Observer* newspaper some years ago. We saw a skinhead running aggressively down a street, a businessman defending himself from attack with a briefcase held up to protect himself from harm as he is flung against the wall of a building by this hooligan. Then the film ran again. For three quarters of it the scene was the same; only at the end did the camera pull up and away to reveal a builder's pallet, full of rubble about to fall. It landed just where the businessman would have been if the youth had not seen the danger and flung him out of harm's way. Each version relayed the facts. It was up to the director of the film, and up to you as the audience, to interpret them in accordance with your beliefs.

I heard a story many years ago, and I failed to pay much attention to it at the time:

The monk was working in his garden when he saw a weary traveller approaching on horseback. The traveller was slumped in the saddle and the horse was plodding slowly, without purpose. The monk bade him good day, and asked if there was anything he could give him. The traveller demanded a glass of water. As he drank he said, 'Tell me, priest, where is the next village?'

'Half a day's journey down the valley,' said the monk.

'Tell me, what are the people like there?'

'What were the people like in the village you have come from?'

'They were dishonest, untrusting and untrustworthy, the most miserable bunch of people. I am glad to be rid of them.'

'I'm sorry to tell you,' said the monk, 'but I think you'll find the people in the next village much the same.'

The next week the monk was working in his garden when he saw another traveller coming down from the hills, tired and dusty but upright in the saddle. The horse, striding with a stronger step, came to a halt beside the garden. The monk bade the traveller good day, and asked if there was anything he could do for him.

'A glass of water would refresh me, and perhaps a little for the horse.'

As they drank he asked, 'Tell me, father, where is the next village?'

'Half a day's journey down the valley.'

'And the people there, father, what are they like?'

'First, tell me ,what were the people like in the village you have left?'

'Ah, they were the most wonderful people. I had only intended to spend a day or two there, but I have spent many months in their kind and hospitable company. I have made many friends there whom I am sad to leave.'

'Do not be too sad,' said the monk, 'I think you will find the people in the next village much the same.'

Francesca and I, like the two travellers, were making different movies from the same scenes, with the same cast. She was putting together a movie that said Adrian Gilpin was self-directed, was not prepared to be manipulated into making decisions that he thought were inherently wrong, and was very focused. My film showed me at the mercy of other people's ridiculous, crass decision-making, constantly being kicked and left unrewarded. Francesca simply did not accept, nor believe in, my model.

It was a 'real life', practical example of the lessons I had been learning theoretically on the programmes, and in the books I had been studying. People who move forward do so because they choose the meanings that they attach to the circumstances around them.

You can look at a single set of circumstances in any number of ways, from any number of camera angles. You can edit it together in any way you like, attach any sound score, use any lighting, make it gloomy and despondent, happy and upbeat – or whatever you choose. The choice is yours. *Film noir* had been my chosen style for my own life story. I decided to stop making those movies.

It was all very well making that decision, but I knew that to make a new kind of film I needed more tools.

Six weeks after we closed the consultancy the TEC came in with a substantial six-figure contract for my research into peak performing teams.

8: BACK TO SCHOOL

This is the true joy of life, the being used for a purpose
recognised by yourself as a mighty one . . . being a force
of nature instead of a feverish, selfish little clod of
ailments and grievances complaining that the world
will not devote itself to making you happy.

GEORGE BERNARD SHAW

Now that my partners had decided that they didn't want to be a part of this new movement, of this shift away from consultancy into teaching people how to think, I found myself once again alone. However, Francesca's intervention caused a massive shift in my own thinking. No longer did I feel that my hand had been forced by my partners' desire to sell the business, but by my desire to discover my true path. It had been easy to blame their lack of vision or courage. It was much harder to face the truth that I had attracted the demise of the business because it did not fit my purpose.

Victim or Catalyst?

I was appalled some months later to get a call from an associate to tell me that my partners were speaking of my 'inappropriate pursuit of my own interests' as the reason for their desire to part company with me. I had never given less than 100 per cent of my time, effort and loyalty to their heritage business and to our joint venture. In fact I habitually gave much more than was ever expected; something that grew from a deep need in me to over-deliver on promises. I had even invested my own money in the Mastery programme because I could not be certain of its immediate value to our business. How could they behave like this?

Then I heard that old familiar voice inside my head, the self-justification which so often sounded like a whine. I had given them 100 per cent and more of my professional effort. I hadn't given my heart and spirit. The spark of excellence – as so often before – was not there.

How attuned people are to this. Most of us have encountered people who cannot be criticised for their input, or indeed for their results – just for their lack of passion and spirit. When passion and spirit are withheld there is no foundation for trust. My partners must have sensed this and it made them nervous. I now recognised that I was at the *cause* of the separation, not at the *effect* of it – the accidental catalyst, not the victim. Consciously I was working with great determination to make the business a success. Subconsciously I was moving in a new direction.

With each day it now becomes clearer to me that we move relentlessly in the direction of our thoughts. 'With our thoughts we create our world' – prophetic words from the Buddha. I was, once again, experiencing in my own life the things I was learning about. Over and over again I was reading about and meeting people who imagined the best and experienced much of it, and people who imagined the worst and found that it came true. I resolved to choose my thoughts with great care.

Now I had no excuse. Now I had every opportunity to do it my way, to follow my own pathway, to build up the teams of people that I wanted around me, and to create an organisation where I wasn't going to be shackled by other people's comfort zones, or held back by other people's fears of failure – my own were going to be hard enough to deal with!

Now I knew where I wanted my road to take me.

As if by magic, within six weeks Kent TEC had said they were willing to invest in our ongoing research and development. Almost on a daily basis I was getting signals that I was making the right decisions about my life. In the past I had pulled together many of the projects through struggle and effort, against the odds. Now, for the first time I was being drawn towards something, rather than having to push things into place for myself. I was beginning to experience a natural flow of the right people and the right resources coming together to support me. The right opportunities were being presented at just the right time and in just the right way. I had a sense of being on a journey, of heading towards something new.

All my teachers had been saying: 'When you know what you want, and when you know why you want it, the "how" reveals itself.' Now I knew for myself that all the way through my earlier career I had been starting at the wrong end of the thinking process.

Learning Addict

With the money that Kent TEC had invested I wanted to translate some of the teaching, heavily influenced by American research, and ideas that had their roots outside the shores of the UK, into a format that was accessible to business and working people in a very different culture. I had to identify the material that was most needed in this country by people wanting to work effectively, by people wanting to set up their businesses effectively, or by big businesses who wanted to unleash the vast opportunities presented by change. Evolution – inevitable and natural change – was viewed by so many as a threat, or an enemy. I wanted to find a way to excite people about change. Change had always meant better things for me in the end – terrible sometimes in the face of it and magnificent after the event. I needed to find how to present and describe it to people so that we would achieve their willing endorsement. I had a lot of learning to do.

The grant funding was the opportunity to go back to school, to invest in learning with a passion and an excitement which I had never had in my formal education.

I explored close to four hundred books, and listened to just over two and a half thousand hours of audiotapes of some of the world's great thinkers commenting on all areas of human activity. I attended seminars on a monthly, sometimes weekly basis, something over three thousand hours in total, investigating areas such as the psychology of achievement, neuro-linguistic programming, the language of influence and persuasion. I met and worked with business practitioners and psychologists in an attempt to find interventions that consistently produced positive change in people's thinking and beliefs. Above all, I spent hundreds of days with like-minded people exploring philosophical, pragmatic, simple, complex and always stimulating ideas.

I developed a voracious appetite to learn about the nature of the people who shape the world in which we live, who shape families, organisations of excellence, the communities in which they are living, and the religions they follow. What was it about these people that was different from the rest of us?

Out of all of this I started to gain some sense of wanting to have a very deep impact on people's lives. I wanted to give people access to the same knowledge base and breadth of wisdom I had been exploring, to wake people up to the possibility of taking command of their lives, of discovering what it is they want to do, and why it is they want to do it; to give them the tools to turn their dreams into reality. What sort of person would I have to become to achieve any of this?

Back to the Future

> *I always wondered, 'Why has nobody discovered me?*
> *In school, didn't they see that I'm more clever than*
> *anybody in this school? That the teachers are stupid,*
> *too? That all they had was information I didn't*
> *need.' It was obvious to me. Why didn't they put me*
> *into art school? Why didn't they train me? I was*
> *different, I was always different. Why didn't anybody*
> *notice me?*
>
> JOHN LENNON

At about this time my father, who was in the process of clearing out much of his own paperwork, dumped on my desk all my old school reports, from the age of four to eighteen. Reading them through I was certain that I would be remembered by my school teachers as someone who was listless, lazy, with a good brain but who couldn't be bothered, someone who never quite lived up to anybody's expectations.

I wondered what memory my school friends would have had of me. The memory of an 'outsider'? Of someone who was pompous and aloof? Of someone who never quite belonged to any group? Of someone who was never fully committed?

That became the starting point for me, to decide how I was going to be remembered by people from now on. I asked myself how I wanted to be remembered by my family, by my work colleagues, by my friends and by people who touched in on the teaching I could make available to them.

When I began to write the answers down, I started to build up a picture of someone whom I only half recognised. I knew that somehow this person had always been what I wanted to be, but all of my efforts so far had produced the antithesis. I was writing down how I wanted to be remembered. I decided that from now on I had to start to live in this way.

9: VALUES, BELIEFS AND THE LANGUAGE OF EXCELLENCE

For as he thinketh in his heart, so is he.

PROVERBS 23:7

What I had written down, these words, was a list of the qualities that I valued most in other people. If I wanted to be remembered by my family as being 'affectionate', 'gentle', 'reliable', 'strong', 'true', these were values. If I wanted to be remembered by my colleagues as 'honest', 'motivating', 'stimulating', 'congruent', these were values. If you ask yourself the question, 'How do I want to be remembered?', you discover some of your deepest driving values, the things that you respond to best in other people and the things that you want people to respond to in you. I wanted people to remember my laughter, my integrity and my courage.

Another question that I was asking myself was 'What are the most important things in life for me?' This opened the floodgates. Family, choice, freedom, excitement, learning, excellence . . . these, too, I valued highly and I wanted them to be the foundations of my future.

Just holding these values to be important doesn't necessarily mean you are living by them. I discovered a huge incongruence between what I saw as valuable, what I respected in other people, what I wanted to be like myself, and my actual *behaviour* over the past years.

Now at least I was beginning to set out an agenda for change. If this was what I wanted to be, and I was not yet like this, I had some clear focus on which areas of my life I needed to develop, which moral, spiritual, metaphysical muscles I needed to build.

The Values Gym

It felt a bit like going to a gym for the first time: in five minutes you discover that you have muscles you didn't even know existed. After a day or two of this mental exercise I began to ache in a much deeper part of me than my physical muscles. I discovered that there were character muscles that I had not exercised, some of them for years. This had produced the inherent lack of congruence inside me that was the probable cause of many of the disruptions of my life and career.

Never before had I mapped out my values with any kind of clarity. These values, surely, were to be the foundations upon which I wanted to build my life. There was much work to be done, but at least I had a plan. Of course, some values were already a key part of my daily life. Others were flabby; and some of them I found hard to find in my behaviour at all. Now I had to find out what it was that enabled people to live by *their* values, by *their* guiding principles. Was it a skill that I needed? Was there some exercise that would enable me to do that? Or was there a deeper thinking process, a deeper part of who I was that I needed to access?

My determination to align my behaviour with my chosen values is still reaffirmed every time I have the opportunity to model great business leaders. Julian Richer's company, Richer Sounds, is now something of a phenomenon. Richer Sounds achieved and held on to the world record of retail sales per square foot six years running in the *Guinness Book of Records*. Every page of Richer's recent book *The Richer Way* explodes with value-centred statements. Every business process described in that book is rooted in Richer's key values.

Integrity

> *What distinguishes the majority of men from the few*
> *is their inability to act according to their beliefs.*
> HENRY MILLER

On the face of it Richer's power comes from this complete congruence between what matters to him and what he does. His personal and business values seem to be an effective power-base for commercial achievement. What intrigued me was how different these values were from the accepted view of a hard-nosed commercial world.

On every page of his book his company's values are transparent. Innovation, freedom, ideas, recognition, loyalty, winning, lifestyle, honesty and continuous improvement are at the top of a phenomenal list of the core principles driving his success.

Charles Dunstone of the Carphone Warehouse is among the most humble of business leaders I met. He once told me with disarming honesty, 'I don't know which of the things I talk about make people tick.' As I listened it became all too obvious why people follow his leadership.

The Carphone Warehouse was established in 1989 with a £6000 investment. By the end of 1996 they had opened 82 shops. The target for the end of 1997 is 140 shops with businesses opening across the globe. Sales have grown from £2 million in 1991 to £106 million in 1997. At the time of writing they have captured an 11 per cent share of all new mobile connections, 41 per cent of all high street connections and 47 per cent of all high street sales by value. Why?

As Dunstone builds the business he does so on solid foundations, on two key sets of values which he calls the rational proposition and the emotional proposition:

RATIONAL PROPOSITION	EMOTIONAL PROPOSITION
Impartiality	Young
Range (of products)	Enthusiastic
Choice	Unconventional
Knowledge	Fast-growing
Meaningful guarantees	Friendly
Integrity	Customer-focused
Recognisable brand	Innovative

Listening to him I realised how highly he valued integrity. Because he wants the customer to enjoy impartial advice, his staff have no hidden incentives to push one network rather than another. Commission paid on a sale is fixed, regardless of the value of the sale to Carphone Warehouse. All company behaviour must be congruent with the published values of the business. This is quite different from a business which trades on customer service and rejects refunds as a matter of policy, or trades on quality and fails to train staff on its processes and systems.

In his presentations Charles Dunstone produces a slide headed, 'We are obsessed by Customer Service'. This is the language of the passionate. When you listen to unstoppable people in business, sport, arts, science or any area of human endeavour you can *feel* their passion bursting out. Go into one of Charles Dunstone's shops or Julian Richer's shops, go into Body Shop or Pret á Manger or Planet Hollywood and feel the passion and the underpinning values that fuel this level of success.

The Beliefs Trail

> *'One can't believe impossible things,' said Alice. 'I daresay you haven't had much practice,' said the Queen. 'When I was your age, I always did it for half-an-hour a day. Why, sometimes I've believed as many as six impossible things before breakfast.'*
> LEWIS CARROLL, *THROUGH THE LOOKING-GLASS*

In business Dunstone believes that integrity of advice and service produces a more sustainable business footing than ripping confused customers off. Julian Richer believes that most employers are still in the Stone Age when it comes to understanding their primary asset – people.

Beyond the world of business Mother Teresa clearly held a different faith from the self-styled religious terrorists who murder innocents in the name of their god. Mother Teresa believed that mankind has been created in the image of God. She clearly had values founded upon her deep religious convictions. Saddam Hussein and other violent military dictators have fundamentally different beliefs about the structure of the world and of humanity, and, therefore, fundamentally different values.

The work of the anthropologist Gregory Bateson, and of American author and teacher Robert Dilts, tells us that our values are consistently underpinned by what we believe. As our beliefs change so we start to value different things.

It was time for me to start reorganising what *I* believed about the world.

Already I was discovering values in me that I *wanted* to live by but was not yet living by. Instead of trying to force them into place by some kind of generalised affirmation, 'Every day, in every way I am more and more congruent, more and more honest', I needed to tackle the *beliefs* which underpinned those values. What did I believe about the structure of the world? What did I believe about other people, and the nature of humanity? What did I believe about myself? What did I believe about success, about failure, about business, about money, about wealth? Did I have a faith in anything beyond the fleshly instability of the human condition?

When I investigated my beliefs with honesty, I started to reveal, layer by layer like peeling an onion, aspects of my inner self that were driving everything I did and everything I achieved. If I was to come face to face with my belief system, I had to have a structured way of looking at it. I started to jot down the key areas of my life. There was my *family*, my *friends*; *relationships* with business colleagues, with the business itself; there was my *financial position*; there were my *talents*, my *skills*, my *career*; my *health* and my *fitness*; the amount of *fun* that I had, the leisure and *recreation*; my beliefs in my *spirituality*, in anything that lay outside my human experience. As I looked at all of these headings, I had one of the most uncomfortable experiences of my life.

The Fear Dragon

> *At eighteen our convictions are hills from which we look; at forty-five they are caves in which we hide.*
>
> F. Scott Fitzgerald

I realised that in every one of those areas I was frightened. I was frightened that my career wouldn't achieve the heights I wanted it to; frightened that I didn't have the skills and capabilities to do all the things I wanted to do; frightened that

I might not sustain close relationships with my friends and family. If I looked at the statistics, there was the fear that maybe even my marriage might not survive. Would my children grow up to love and respect me, or would they be describing Francesca and me in the same tones of frustration that most people use when they talk about their parents?

There was the fear that this month, next month, the month after there might be no more money, no more work, that I might not be able to continue to pay for my children's education, that I might never be able to provide the house and the holidays and the qualities of life that were important to me and my family. There was the fear that, if I didn't take more notice of my health and fitness, everything else could be going well and I could keel over at the age of fifty with heart disease.

This extraordinary fear of failure permeated every aspect of my life. Each time I thought about what it was I wanted to achieve there was a churning feeling inside my stomach. What would it be like if, one day, I had to accept that I was never going to make it in that area?

> *He has not learned the lesson of life who does not*
> *every day surmount a fear.*
> RALPH WALDO EMERSON

As I reflected on the challenging lessons I had undergone in the incredibly intense period of my studies, I realised just how debilitating that fear, that underlying belief that things might not turn out all right, would be – how debilitating it already was. If I was frightened about not having the skills and capabilities to do what I wanted to do, then I wasn't going to do it, I wasn't going to take the risk. If I was frightened about not being able to provide financially for my family, then I was going to avoid any sort of financial risk. If I was frightened about the strength of my relationship with my wife then I might be subconsciously engendering mistrust in one of the most important parts of my life. If I was frightened that my children wouldn't grow up to like and to love me, then I might be creating the failure simply by anticipating it. My fears would become self-fulfilling prophecies.

> *Every time a child says, 'I don't believe in fairies,'*
> *there is a fairy somewhere that falls down dead.*
> SIR J. M. BARRIE

Taming the Dragon

> *The man who has ceased to fear has ceased to care.*
> F. H. BRADLEY

From studies of the attitude of teachers to pupils in schools and of managers to high-flyers within organisations I knew that people quickly fulfil the expectations being made of them. If one teacher is told that Simon is a gifted child and Sally is a slow learner, the teacher observes these characteristics, behaves accordingly and catalyses high levels of achievement from Simon and disappointing results from Sally. If another teacher is briefed differently and observes Sally as gifted and Simon as slow, the results will be reversed.

In a ground-breaking book on this subject, *Leadership and the New Science*, Margaret Wheatley confirmed, 'If a manager is told that a new trainee is particularly gifted, that manager will see genius emerging from the trainee's mouth even in obscure statements. But if the manager is told his or her new hire is a bit slow on the uptake, the manager will interpret a brilliant idea as a sure sign of sloppy thinking or obfuscation.'

I decided that from now on I had to choose very carefully what I wanted to believe about myself, my marriage, my children, my career, the world, money, abundance. I would choose new beliefs. I would go out and find the evidence to support them. Instead of my belief system being based on what I had acquired by accident from other people over the last forty years of my life, I would now go out and choose to pay attention to the evidence that would support the beliefs that I wanted to hold.

After all, this is what we are doing anyway. Anybody who believes, and has a deep faith in Christianity, will pay attention to the evidence that supports that belief. They will pay attention to the work of Mother Teresa and other leading Christian workers, to the good works of the Churches around the globe, to miracles and the evidence that has been made manifest over the last two thousand years. People who choose not to believe in Christianity will pay attention to the corruption in the Church, the behaviour of the Papacy throughout the major events of history, to the observed fact that there are many people who believe in the Christian God and lead a miserable existence. Somebody who wants to follow the Hindu faith will pay attention to the benefits that the Hindu faith brings to many of its practitioners. People who want to argue with that belief will pay attention to Hinduism's eccentricities and failings.

Man is what he believes.
ANTON CHEKHOV

It seemed to me sensible, rather than allowing it to happen by accident, or by unwittingly giving sanction to part of your mother's or your father's belief system, or part of what is said on television news programmes, to choose your own belief system very, very carefully, and then look for the evidence that will enable you to support that belief. Anthony Robbins describes a belief as an idea with legs. You start with an idea and look for evidence to support that idea by bringing in supporting experiences, by attaching legs to all four corners. You can end up with a belief like a solid table top with impenetrable legs of proof and evidence.

> *We are what we think. All that we are arises with our*
> *thoughts. With our thoughts, we make our world.*
> THE BUDDHA

It seemed to me that what I had to do now was to make a commitment to living my life in accordance with deliberately chosen, empowering beliefs. If we experience the world pretty much as we believe it to be, I might as well decide what I wanted to believe and design my world accordingly.

> *If you think you can or think you can't you are right.*
> HENRY FORD

More than anything I dreaded finding myself in a rocking-chair aged ninety-nine with the words, 'If only . . .', nagging at the memories of my life. I would no longer allow my beliefs to limit me. Delays, mistakes, disappointments – I could live with all of these. I could not live with regret; I would banish all possibility of regret.

Of all sad words of tongue or pen
The saddest are these: "It might have been"!
JOHN GREENLEAF WHITTIER

10: Whose Truth Is It Anyway?

People are always blaming their circumstances for what
they are. I don't believe in circumstances. The people
who get on in this world are the people who get up and
look for the circumstances they want, and, if they can't
find them, make them.

George Bernard Shaw

Three quarters of me was now believing that our daily experience of this world was dictated and governed by our belief system. We experience what we believe to be true. Yet, there was still part of me with this nagging doubt. 'It's all very well, but if I am knocked down by a bus, it's no good saying, "I believe I can walk"!' Then I would remember the thousands of stories of people who have done just that; the people who have thought their way out of cancer, out of paralysis, out of all kinds of extraordinary, terminal conditions.

I remembered a powerful experience in America, listening to a woman called Kathy Buckley, whose full story is too long to tell in these pages. She was the victim of an appalling childhood. She was deaf, and she was dumb. She was treated very harshly. She was abused by her family and by the institutions which were supposed to protect her. Twice in her life she was diagnosed as having cancer and told she had only a few weeks to live. She was run over while she was sleeping on a beach, unable to hear the approaching Land Rover, and her spine was snapped. She was told she would never walk again.

On every one of these occasions the character that was Kathy Buckley simply refused to be told what to do, to kow-tow to these assaults on her body and spirit. Now she is a fit and healthy and walking individual, still stone-deaf, earning her living as a comedienne on the club platforms of America.

One of the finest teachers that I had the privilege of working with was Robert Dilts, author of many authoritative books on genius, leadership and change. His mother was diagnosed as having advanced cancer which had penetrated her bone marrow. Her doctors made the judgement that there was little that could be done and advised her to prepare for the worst. She refused to accept the prognosis and turned to her son and his work around beliefs and changing beliefs. She was able to send the cancer into remission and she bought herself a further thirteen years of active life.

In his book, *Chicken Soup for the Soul*, Mark Victor Hansen tells the tale of Patti Wilson. As a young child coping with epilepsy, she decided that she wanted to 'break the chains on the brains that limit so many people', and set herself the goal of breaking the long-distance running record for women. The furthest any woman had run up to then was 80 miles. Patti's first marathon was 400 miles. On her seventeenth birthday she completed a 1,500-mile marathon, and she finally crossed the United States from the East coast to the West and was met by the President. Her fund-raising efforts have financed 19 multi-million-dollar epilepsy centres around America. Patti simply believed she *could*, and she believed there is no more powerful example of leadership than giving people the chance to change their beliefs about what is possible.

Joseph Jaworski writes in *Synchronicity – The Inner Path of Leadership* of his work with the American Leadership Forum and later with Shell. He believes that deep and sustainable corporate and community transformation can best, or indeed only, be led when the change is facilitated by people who have experienced deep personal transformation. This process of transformation begins when the individual is willing to face the beliefs that set the limits of change. Jaworski's current work with major corporations on the impact of scenario-planning differs from anything else I have encountered because it takes as its first supposition that when key people can be led to believe in a particular future scenario, the vision is all but certain. The process of creating the vision creates the future.

This is a major shift of belief for most people in business and touches on some of the most exciting, and difficult to comprehend, work being done by quantum scientists. Jaworski describes these processes better than anyone else in the business arena; he can do so because he knows the process internally. This is something many of our business and community leaders would do well to emulate.

Struggling with this question of whether it is possible to think oneself into or out of anything, I reread the work of the new scientists. All of the theories about the mechanical nature of this universe that I had learned at school were being completely rewritten by a new generation of scientists. Early in the twentieth century scientists started to look at the structure of the universe in a radically different way. When they were able to study subatomic particles in detail they began to realise that the very process of observation in an experiment would determine the results of that experiment. The process of observation interfered with the experiment itself.

They began to come up with highly complex and difficult theories, some of which no one fully understands yet, but there was a strong movement to suggest that, not just philosophically but quite literally, as we think so we create the world. If a scientist, observing a subatomic experiment, changes his thinking during the course of the experiment, the experiment changes, too. The work of physicists and biochemists, possibly for the first time in the history of the world, is beginning to support the philosophy and theology of some of the greatest thinkers. We are beginning to find explanations for coincidence, explanations for miracles, explanations for the uncanny and the apparently supernatural. It is even possible that the combined thinking of humanity within this universe is co-creating this universe.

Maybe it is literally true that the life that you experience is the life that you *think*. Programmes have shown that if one of a group of long-term unemployed people starts to think differently, then she or he is the one who suddenly starts to make changes in their life. If one of the group describes *himself* as redundant while another starts to describe how *her job* was made redundant, then the one who describes the job as redundant will quickly move on to something else, while the other remains redundant in the society in which he operates.

The way we describe the world to ourselves, the things we believe to be true, just become true. The world is the way we describe it to ourselves. If these underlying beliefs that underpin our values are the critical drivers, the co-creators of our experience of this world, it doesn't matter whether we are right, or whether we are wrong. We are going to experience the world pretty much as we *think* it is.

It seemed to me vitally important not only to decide what I wanted my beliefs to be. I had to start to look for specific evidence to support those beliefs so that I could have confidence in them, so that they could become a faith. It seemed vitally important that, on a daily basis, I described the world as I wanted it to be.

Just as I was beginning to think in this way I came across the study of linguistics, from Wittgenstein's work through to Noam Chomsky's and many of their disciples and pupils. The underlying message was *that with our language we create our experience of the world, not comment upon our experience of the world.* For instance, if I encounter a failure or a catastrophe and I describe it in those terms I will feel bad about my failure, believe the experience to be catastrophic. If I describe a catastrophe as a nightmare, then it will take on nightmarish qualities and haunt me. If I start to describe the same circumstance as a challenge, an opportunity to learn, a feedback, then I become challenged, I become curious about those opportunities, I start listening to the feedback.

Living Nightmares

I was at this point in my new thinking, when Francesca and I and the three children went on holiday to Greece. Like it or not, there was plenty of evidence to suggest to me that my three were the clumsiest children in the world. There had never been a mealtime at which one, often two, sometimes all three, had not managed to spill their glasses of water, and the ketchup bottle, and most of the contents of their plates over the table – and usually over me too. This belief that I had bred the three clumsiest children in the world reached a peak in Greece.

For months and months and months, I had been giving the children an appallingly hard time every time we went out, particularly if we went to a pub and particularly if we sat at a picnic table. They had a genius for putting their drinks down precisely on the crack between the slats of the picnic table. They didn't even have to look at the table, or the bottle, or me. With seemingly artless precision they ensured that the bottle always toppled in my direction.

On every occasion they did this, mopping furiously I would demand of them why they were so clumsy. I would berate them, and threaten them with sanctions. I built up a belief, and transferred the certainty to the whole family, that *it was impossible to go out for a meal without me becoming subjected to a soaking.*

We were already having a fairly stressful first week of a two-week holiday. We had the usual number of spillages. We had had ice creams down my front; we had had ice creams on the sand, most of the tavernas in the village were bringing out the cloths and the sponges on the same tray as the Cokes.

I had developed a neurotic defence mechanism against this inevitability. As soon as I sat down at a table I would sweep every bottle, every glass, every conceivable container on to my side of the table, leaving a yawning gulf between them and the children. When one of the children wanted a drink they would have to ask for it, and keep both hands underneath the table top until I had passed it across my body and set it down before them, making sure wherever possible that it pointed away from me. The moment they had finished their sip, hands back under the table, and I would return the container to my lair.

Francesca would look at me, long and patient, but despairing at the thought of decades of mealtimes with a neurotic obsessive to cope with, as well as three butter-fingered children.

That particular evening she had, through her fixed smile, intimated that knowing what I had recently been banging on about, about beliefs creating the world in which we live, if I went on telling our children that they were clumsy, that is precisely what they would become. Loath, as always, to learn from my own pupils, I was not listening. My performance that evening reached heights of absurdity that I did not know I could aspire to. I was moving glasses and bottles and plates around the table like a maniac, reinforcing my belief at every moment that this was a good process because *nobody* spilled *anything*. We had kept the sluice-gates closed for two whole courses. My finger was triumphantly in the dyke.

Greece is not the best place to defy the gods, or to indulge in hubris. The Furies are always there, lurking around the corner of even the most welcoming taverna, no respecters of the smug parent. The children, who were already accustomed to the notion that their father, though basically harmless, was not entirely there when it came to meals in restaurants, had resignedly ignored my sweeps and lunges and strange crouchings over my bottle hoard, but sensing I was, for once at a mealtime, in a good mood, asked if they could get down.

'Yes, children,' I beamed, triumphant, 'you have been so good. What excellent children you have been. You have behaved beautifully. Your manners have been wonderful. There have been no spills, no upsets. Of course you can get down while Mummy and Daddy finish their coffee.'

All three children, brimming over with this new-found praise, leaped from their seats, and rushed excitedly to give Daddy a hug. The Furies moved in. The children, swarming around a father who now seemed well fed rather than fed up, swept into their hugs all the bottles, and all the glasses, and deposited them in a seismic flood on to my lap. For a moment I sat, rigid and dripping in the shocked silence, and then an inner dam burst. I fell about laughing. I hadn't laughed so long and so loud for years. The Furies smiled grimly, and moved on, honour satisfied.

Here were the gods, here was the universe playing a joke, telling me to grow up and behave, and be congruent with what I wanted to teach. All of us wept with laughter as the tolerant Greek waiters ushered the Furies out and applied the sponges.

From that moment to this day I have not noticed if my children have spilled their drinks or not. I have no idea whether they are average, above average or below average in the clumsy stakes, because I simply don't notice. I suspect that they *were* above average, certainly while I was reminding them of the fact every time we went out for a meal. I suspect that now they are below average because it is simply irrelevant. At any rate I cannot remember another time that any of my children spilled a drink over me.

Later, I was telling this story in a seminar. While I was telling the story – with perhaps too much theatrical emphasis on the clumsiness – I must have bumped into my stool, tripped, or dropped pens half a dozen times. This created enormous entertainment for my seminar audience, watching me blundering about talking about clumsiness, totally unaware that I was becoming appallingly unwieldy as I did so. Normally I am reasonably co-ordinated on the platform, but for the rest of that afternoon I couldn't walk from one side of the room to the other without dropping something, or knocking into something as I stooped to retrieve whatever I had dropped.

The next day they made me aware of it and it became a running joke for the rest of the seminar, until the following lunchtime. While we were jesting about it one of the delegates started to tell how exactly the same thing had happened to her. Over a period of about six months her husband began to describe her as ham-fisted and clumsy. He would say, 'You know, you can't walk from one side of the room to the other without tripping over. You can't carry anything without dropping it. What is the matter with you?'

It reached the point at which she was so neurotic about it that every time she tried anything she stumbled, fumbled, tore and bumped into things. After a while they had a blazing row. She demanded that he stopped talking about it; it was just the way she was, and he was going to have to live with it. He stopped mentioning it and the phenomenon disappeared immediately and was never apparent again.

She finished her story, both of us pleased that her experience had supported mine, and turned away from us to walk through into lunch. At the door she tripped over the sill, flew headlong, and stumbled on all fours into the dining room.

With our thinking we create our experiences. As Deepak Chopra says in his seminars, 'With our language we create the world.'

Our beliefs, the supporting experiences, and the language we use to describe our beliefs about the world are interrelated. As we shake up this cocktail of what we believe to be true and how we describe it, to all intents and purposes that is what we will experience.

How many times have you told yourself that you couldn't remember the name you were trying to think of, and you were absolutely right? How many times, on the other hand, have you said, 'It'll come to me in a minute', and you were absolutely right? How many times have you been made angry by a person or event, with good cause because you described it to yourself in a certain way, and on another occasion somebody described the same event to you in a different way and it made you laugh?

The same situation that makes you angry can also make you laugh. The same situation that makes you sad can also make you happy. The same situation that can make you consider yourself a failure can also make you consider that you have huge courage, to be able to fail and move on to the next thing. Which of those ideas is true?

The one that you choose.

It is at this point that many of you are going to stop reading this book!

Many people do not want to internalise responsibility for their lives to this extent. They want to believe that the external world is responsible for their experience of it, that it is other people, and other things, and other events that have made all the circumstances of their lives happen. They were just unlucky.

Those of you who are going to become unstoppable in the pursuit of your destiny will read on.

Which category are you now in?

If you are still with me – it may be encouraging to know that, in this field, none of the people who are thinking about this and writing about this yet have the full picture. None of us can fully understand it yet, but we know that this is the way the thinking is going, and our own experiences suggest that this is true. But so far, of course, a smaller number of people believe this than believe what everybody else does. Unstoppable people are in a minority.

So, are you reading on to the next chapter? Or are you deciding to leave it here?

You choose.

11: Me and My Shadow

The way to do is to be.

Lao Tzu

Who Am I?

Here I was revisiting the images of myself at school, at work as an actor and stage manager, running West End theatres, consulting to organisations, building and managing tourist attractions. It was obvious that the Adrian I saw in each of these scenes was so different. Which one was the real Adrian? Who *was* Adrian Gilpin?

Somehow I had been reinventing myself at regular periods throughout my life. I had been a son, a brother, a child, a teenager, an actor, a stage manager, a businessman, an entrepreneur, a consultant, a lover, husband and father. None of these was *who I was*, but *what I did*, the rôles I played. What or who lay at the heart of all this? What were my foundations?

What sort of person was I designing on all those pieces of paper on which I had scribbled my thinking, my values and my beliefs? What new version was I inventing now? What would I have to believe to hold true to these values? What sort of person must I now become, to believe these things and live in this way?

This was the time when I first understood that what we experience in this life has, ultimately, less to do *with what we do*, more to do with *who we are*.

As I read and reread my notes I started to come alive. I was staring at a blueprint for someone new, that person I had always wanted to become. These were the beliefs that I truly wanted to believe. These things were not true yet, but what I was designing was the Adrian Gilpin that had only existed in my dreams until now.

I felt I was drawing near to the core of Adrian Gilpin. 'Who is he?' I was asking. 'He's not what he does: he's not his job; he's not his job title; he's not his behaviour; he's not his health habits; he's not his friends; he's not the house he lives in; he's not the mistakes he makes or the successes he has. Who and where is this Adrian Gilpin?'

He is the identity that lies beyond, or beneath, or at the core of these values that he holds.

It is *that* which makes him unique. Our behaviour can be like other people's behaviour, our jobs can be like other people's jobs, our salaries can be like other people's salaries, our holidays, our tastes, our habits can be like other people's, but that cocktail of values that we choose and shake up for ourselves is unique. Some of the ingredients will be shared by other people, but that particular blend, that particular mix, is unique.

I might believe a number of things that you believe, but not believe others. You might believe a number of the things that I believe, but not believe others. My unique combination of beliefs and values is who I am. That mix is what makes my identity. That is what makes me different from everybody else who has ever lived on this planet.

This is how you come face to face with your own image. This is you. All your values, and all your beliefs, are the blueprint for your identity, your character that lies within.

Sow a character, reap a destiny.
SAMUEL SMILES

Why Me?
The next question was 'Why?'

'Why am I here, with this unique cocktail of beliefs and values? Why is Adrian Gilpin?'

I didn't know how to answer this. There was a blank sheet. All through my life people had been asking me, 'What are you going to do? What do you want to do?' Some had even been telling me what I ought to be doing, and how I should be doing it. My search was no longer about what I should be doing – that wasn't the heart of it. There was more. Much more.

I was becoming conscious of a new belief – that we all have a purpose, a unique reason for being where we are and who we are. I still don't know whether everyone comes to understand what their purpose is, but I believe that there is a reason why each of us is here. The pathway to discovering our purpose seemed to be the question, 'Why me?' For me, there was no answer – just a blank canvas.

This is not a question you can answer in a day or even a year. I think it is something you discover over the rest of your life, but only after you have asked the question. I believe you discover your destiny rather than design it. You can start to prepare yourself for it, and start to map it out. This preparation is what I had been doing, asking myself questions about my values and my beliefs. Perhaps that was my first attempt at it. Appearing now were the first sketches, the first line drawings of who it was I was becoming, who it was I wanted to become.

What was taking shape was a picture of my journey to my destiny, rather than a portrait of my destiny itself.

The Journey Is the Destiny

Over the next years of my life the canvas would take on new and changing colours and tones, the scenes would change, the picture would build, new elements would be drawn in while some would be painted over. I was starting to paint a living canvas of who I wanted to be and why.

The words 'guide', 'teacher', 'mentor', 'coach', kept cropping up in my descriptions of who I wanted to be. This was not very surprising. I had spent so much time with people I would describe in those terms. I had spent time with great teachers, with inspiring mentors, with motivating masters of business, relationships, communication, parenting, creative thinking. I had seen the skill that all these masters had at teaching, and their passion to transfer their knowledge and their experiences. Their stories, questions and guidance were given in an attempt to draw out of me, their pupil, my own excellence. Their purpose seemed to be to help me understand where I was going.

I liked that. It was compelling. It was a thrilling way to live, studying the thinking, the beliefs and the values, the habits and the attitudes of extraordinary people, and learning from them. If in the process I was able to start doing things well, reaching for my own excellence, then I could continue in their tradition, and continue to teach and to coach.

As I stared at this blank canvas a shape started to emerge around this concept of guiding. I remembered that one of the most engaging books I had read as a teenager was *The Lord of the Rings* by J. R. R. Tolkien. From the earliest age I can remember I have always been fascinated by the process of magic and change. When I was still at school I used to earn my living in the holidays as a conjuror at children's parties or in cabaret, rather than working in a factory or a shop.

I remembered Gandalf from *The Lord of the Rings*, his wizardry and his ability to be present at the right time, in the right place, for the people whose lives he was impacting. But by the end of the book the character I most identified with was Strider. Gandalf had been a key protagonist in *The Hobbit*, and it was Gandalf that most of us wanted to stay with to the end of the story. However, Gandalf's rôle started to diminish in *The Lord of the Rings* and Strider arrived; a grey man, a traveller, a man who was difficult to know, cloaked, silent and private.

As the story progressed Strider took on a stronger and stronger rôle, in support of the quest to which the rest of the characters were committed. He didn't appear to be leading it. It wasn't his quest. He was just there, supporting the others on their journey. Without him the quest would not have succeeded, but he never claimed leadership, he never claimed power. He was simply there – a servant.

It was only right at the end of the tale that you discovered just who he was. He was the rightful King, who had been disguised, and who had been serving all the others in the successful completion of their quest. Only then could he rightfully take his place. The modesty, the disguise, the anonymity really appealed to me and I found that very compelling. There was the man who spent his journey as the servant, so that he could take his place as the leader. He was the pure Servant Leader, one of many examples in mythology.

Joseph Jaworski believes that 'the ultimate aim of the servant leader's quest is to find the resources of character to meet his or her destiny'. I was beginning to understand the journey I was on. For most of my life I had been very good at pushing myself to the front, demanding my share, seeking the credit and position. Now I was learning how to serve, how to guide the quests and journeys of others.

> *There is one quality which one must possess to win,*
> *and that is definiteness of purpose, the knowledge of*
> *what one wants, and a burning desire to possess it.*
>
> NAPOLEON HILL

If I was to discover my true reason for being here it was not up to me to define this in fixed and finite terms. I was setting sail on a journey of discovery, and that journey had to be in service to other people on the same pathway. We all have a different purpose, we all have a different quest, we all have a different reason for being here. Perhaps, the only way to discover my purpose was to facilitate other people on their journey to the same point. If I could help other people to find their reason for being, then I might be given the same gift of knowing mine.

For the first time in my life, I knew what I wanted to do.

I wanted to immerse myself in whatever wisdom I could find, then speak of it in my own voice, my own style. I wanted to interpret it in my own way, and to make it available to other people. By teaching people I would learn more: by learning more I could teach more. By guiding other people I would be guided to my own destiny.

It was no longer a question of *going out* to find the resources I needed to make all this possible. It was a question of *discovering inside* me what I had to give. I began to recognise that we are born with all the qualities, all the skills, all the character we need to achieve our own destiny, but we have to discover it – and unleash it – for ourselves. We have to go out and find our own mentors and teachers who enable us to recognise for ourselves what riches and power lie within. That power can be awesome and I think we often fear it as much as we fear our weaknesses.

> *Our deepest fear is not that we are inadequate. Our deepest fear is that we are powerful beyond measure. It is our light, not our darkness, which frightens us most.*
>
> MARIANNE WILLIAMSON, *A RETURN TO LOVE*

I now believed that the resources I needed to realise my own destiny were inherent within me. I didn't yet have the tools, I didn't have the insights, the wisdom or the experience to know how to unleash these resources. So I had to find teachers. To find the best teachers, I had to teach. To find my own resources I had to help other people to find theirs. Each time I unleashed something in someone else, so I might find a way of unleashing something in me.

It is the process of teaching that reveals to us what it is we most need to learn. Now, every time I stand on a platform I hear myself doing it. Often, when I become most passionate, and have finished an inspiring, motivating, passionate discourse on a subject, I think to myself, 'H'mm, now isn't that interesting? It's me I've been talking to.'

12: MARKERS AND MILESTONES

'Would you tell me, please, which way I ought to go
from here?'
'That depends a good deal on where you want to get to,'
said the Cat.
'I don't much care where,' said Alice.
'Then it doesn't matter which way you go,' said the Cat.

LEWIS CARROLL, *ALICE'S ADVENTURES IN WONDERLAND*

A t least, by asking questions I had a canvas, though I was still a long way from achieving clarity. In fact I was beginning to feel that maybe the full picture might only be revealed to us as we 'shuffle off this mortal coil'.

I believed then, as I believe now, that each of us has a unique purpose, and it is a great one. That purpose becomes revealed to us, in a tantalising and mysterious way, only when we are ready to recognise it, and courageous enough to accept any of the tasks it reveals to us.

It seemed also, from reading the autobiographies of the great achievers, that success comes most easily to people when they understand their purpose. Now I needed to create a pathway through my life with measuring points along the way, marker posts, or milestones to aim for. Achieving these would help to reveal to me more of my purpose, more of my gifts, more of my reason for being.

One of the key lessons that were coming out of reading so many of my teachers was that they had conditioned themselves to be purposeful in almost everything they thought and everything they did. If our desire is to discover our key purpose for being here, it seemed that we should condition ourselves to be purpose-full, *full* of purpose.

The best way of doing that is to condition your mind to know precisely why you are asking every question you ask, to know why you are doing everything you do, to know what it is you want to achieve, what milestones and marker posts you want to reach and pass. Then you must develop a structured way of thinking about these milestones, these desires, these dreams, these goals, whether they are material ones, or experiential ones or spiritual ones. Whatever we desire, if we have a purposeful way of setting about reaching it we will be more successful than if we don't.

So, how do we get ourselves thinking in a purposeful way, on a daily basis?

The starting point is to set specific desires, specific goals. Then comes the problem of overcoming the fear dragon which blocks the path to the successful achievement of them.

The fear that lurks beneath your desire to achieve, the fear about finances, about career, about attaining anything you desire, is caused by many things, but most of all by the huge gap there appears to be between our present reality and the reality we desire. Here we are, surrounded by evidence that this is the way the world is, the evidence that this is the money that is, or isn't, in the bank, by the reality of relationships, or of our career so far. The desired reality of the world that we wish, the world that we dream about, seems so far removed from that, that when we ask the question, 'How are we going to achieve this?', by definition there is, as we have seen, no 'how'.

Yet some people do manage to close the gap between the present reality and the desired reality. How do they do that? What are the processes that they use?

This became my new obsession. It was all very well knowing we should be purposeful, and that people who know their purpose and are purpose*ful* get what they want. There seemed to be something more than that. There seemed to be a dynamic happening in this place that I call the 'reality gap'.

The Reality Gap

I started looking at the whole psychology of desire and goals. I came across the concept of 'cognitive dissonance' which holds that you cannot sustain in your mind simultaneously two opposing realities, two opposing sets of facts about the world. The subconscious mind is designed and programmed to close that gap, to resolve any dissonance between one reality and another reality. This process is an automatic and very basic function of our psychology.

That was all very well, but I had been well aware in my past that I had set a goal, had a shot at it, maybe had a second shot at it to prove that everything I had done the first time wasn't going to work a second time either. If I was really determined I might have had a third shot at it if only to convince myself absolutely that there was no point in trying again.

What happened was that the goal started to shrink, to become smaller and smaller, less and less significant, as it moved closer and closer to my present reality. There was a movement there, an energy, something was happening, but it was happening in the wrong direction. On the other hand, there have been other times in my life when the actual process of setting the goal meant that my present reality suddenly caught up with it, and everything around me became like the reality I had desired.

Clearly there was a movement in both directions. It was possible to dream a dream and then make that dream smaller and smaller and smaller each time I failed to achieve it; and equally possible to find that my present reality was changing and shifting to catch up with, and be like, my desired reality. There was a huge energy flow, as if present reality was attached to a far distant desired reality by a length of elastic, or a giant rubber band.

Dynamic Tension

As my dreams started to become greater and greater, the tension that built inside me was tangible. My image of the rubber band became a powerful aid to my thinking about goals. I imagined one end of the band attached to present reality and the other end attached to desired reality. As the two moved apart, tension built in the rubber.

As I dreamed more and more about what I desired, the tension became so strong that I could imagine the rubber band moving in any one of a number of directions. The desire-end of the band could snap back to present reality, or the present-end could accelerate forward to the desired reality and all of my dreams come true, or, as in most cases, I could let go of both ends at the same time and the rubber band could fall to the middle ground, giving me something of what I wanted, but not all. This seems to be the pattern that I had always run and, indeed, that most people run. Most of us move forward to some degree – but rarely in line with our larger dreams.

When I set myself an ambitious goal, suddenly imagining a business project or a concept that was way beyond anything that I had experienced before or had resources for, my stomach churned. The tensions were palpable inside my body, just as the tensions are palpable within the rubber band.

So, how did I get rid of those tensions? How did I start to clear myself from the stress of the fear of failure?

The tension in the rubber band is simply stored energy. I thought, 'I don't want to get rid of this energy, this tension that is building up inside me. I want to convert that real physical and psychological tension into the energy that moves me towards my desired reality, to make sure that when I release that energy I am moving towards my desired reality, and I am not simply lessening my goals or weakening my dreams.'

I looked at all of the literature, particularly from the 1960s and 1970s, about positive thinking and positive mental attitudes and affirmations. This was interesting stuff. It was entirely consistent with so many of the things that I was discovering about moving in the direction of our thoughts, but it didn't seem to be the whole picture.

It seemed that, just as when we *believe* something to be true we *experience* the world in that way, the same is true of goal-setting. The question I was asking was 'When we release that stored energy, how can we be sure that the direction of movement is *towards* our desired reality, and not back down into our current reality?'

Dominant Thoughts

It seemed to me that the energy of the rubber band would move towards the dominant image we hold in our consciousness. Just as in our beliefs, if we can hold an image of success in our mind's eye, and if that image is more rich and more colourful, and more dominant and more compelling and more detailed than the image that we hold in our mind's eye about our current state of affairs, then our whole psychology, our whole neurophysiology, is conditioned to move us in that direction when we release the energy.

How, then, can we construct a process, a way of mental conditioning, to make that happen more often than not, so that we can build these compelling images in our mind's eye?

The problem is that we are surrounded every day by strong visual input about our current state of affairs. If we have no money and are living in what we believe to be a hovel, if we have no relationships, or a bad relationship, if we have no money in our bank account, we can see the evidence of that. The amount of input from our current reality is overwhelming. That is why most of us sit around saying, 'Well, look at me, how can I possibly move from here? I have no money, I have no relationship, I have no job.' The evidence is overwhelming, and it conditions our thinking every moment of every day.

How, then, do we override that? How do we start to plant inside our subconscious an image of the desire, the goal, the dream, that is even stronger than the evidence around us? That was the task I set myself.

Setting the Focus

I knew by now that all of the evidence of psychological research over the last fifty years and more was that people who attained what they wanted were able to create not only the belief systems to support it, but such a clarity of dream that, to all intents and purposes, it was more real than the reality of their daily lives.

From a lot of the work that I was doing with Dr Tad James, the developer of Time Line Therapy™ in the States, I learned that one of the prime characteristics of the subconscious mind is that it cannot tell the difference between what you have experienced and what you have imagined with emotional intensity. When you go to see a horror movie your conscious mind knows perfectly well that you are safe, and yet you hold your breath and clutch the arms of your seat, and then you leap out of your skin. If you have a phobia about moths, your conscious mind knows perfectly well that moths are not going to harm you or hurt you, but your subconscious mind produces involuntary responses, so that you sweat, you shake with terror, despite the fact that your conscious mind knows that you are behaving like a small child.

Because your subconscious cannot tell the difference between direct, experiential input and what it is imagining with emotional intensity, you can watch a love story, or a movie about cartoon creatures encountering some emotional trauma, and you shed a tear with them. The subconscious mind, which is overwhelmingly powerful, is behaving as if it is real.

'The End in Mind'

Over the last twenty-five years a lot of the work in the

psychology of achievement and the psychology of excellence has been looking at how achievers build a visualisation in their mind's eye that convinces them, at the psychological level, that they have already achieved their goals. If you are Linford Christie, and you are about to run a race, the images that you have in your mind's eye are not images of the discussion you had with your spouse that morning, or the discussion with your bank manager that if you do not win this race then he is not going to extend your overdraft facility, or images about the fact that the guy running in the lane next to you has beaten you in the last three encounters you have had with him. You have an image in your mind's eye of what it is like to be on the far side of the finishing line.

When high-performance athletes are faced with a challenge and are performing at their peak they have a very powerful image in their mind's eye of what it is like to be beyond the finish. They are starting the event 'with the end in mind', as Stephen Covey says. If you are Roger Bannister, and you're the first person to run a four-minute mile in a recorded race, you will have succeeded by conditioning a belief that you have already done it. Consciously, of course, you know perfectly well that you haven't done it yet: subconsciously, you can *rehearse the process to the point where you believe that it has already happened.* In this moment you are conditioning a powerful part of your mind to operate as if it had already successfully achieved the goal.

I remember dreaming that one day I would be famous.
JACKIE STEWART

The framework was there. Now I wanted to find out what,

precisely, these high achievers were doing. Many of the training programmes I had been through in my business career had taught the power of positive thinking, and positive affirmation. Simply standing in front of a mirror saying, 'Every day, in every way, I get more and more beautiful', doesn't actually achieve very much for most people, most of the time, but it is an important starting point. The positive affirmation, constructing the goal as I call it, is the first stage.

Constructing the Goal

If you write the goal in the first person, present tense, in a positive emotional frame – if you write, 'I am free to do the things that excite me now that I own my own house outright' – you are creating a desired reality. You are writing about it as if it were already present. That seems to be the consistent pattern used by achievers over the years. They don't write goals in the future tense, because their subconscious mind knows they haven't got it yet, it's still 'over there', just as well as their conscious mind knows they haven't got it yet, it's still 'over there'. Conscious and subconscious minds are in complete agreement, there is no tension between the two, and you operate as you know the world to be. You operate as though you haven't achieved your goal yet.

Even if your conscious mind knows you have a heavy mortgage, and you still limit many of your choices because of your lack of financial independence, your subconscious can be conditioned into thinking that you have already achieved the freedom that excites you. Then there is a tension between the two. Now, at the subconscious level there is a desired reality different from the present reality and there is a conflict. The theory of cognitive dissonance says you can't hold those two beliefs in one mind. One of them has to shift. Writing your goals in the first person, present tense, positive frame is the first step to conditioning your thinking to be goal-orientated, to be outcome-orientated, to be starting 'with the end in mind'.

Records of Achievement

The process of writing the goal down makes a commitment at a deeper subconscious level than if you simply dream. A study of Harvard graduates over a number of years divided them into two camps at the end of the experiment: those who had achieved everything they had set out to achieve, or who had achieved more; and those who had achieved less, or hadn't even got on to the starting blocks. Clearly, the difference between the two groups had nothing to do with their academic abilities or intellectual capacities since they were all Harvard MBAs. Some of it may have had something to do with bad luck, or misfortune, but since most had had some bad luck and some good it didn't seem to be anything to do with that.

One of the key differences was that every single one of the group who had achieved everything they had set out to achieve, or more, were recording their life's experience on a regular basis. They left Harvard University with a written life plan, written down before they left. Many of them had not followed that plan. They continued to rewrite the plan every time they changed their mind. They wrote about their successes, and their learning experiences. They wrote about when they were moving towards what they wanted, and when they were moving away from what they wanted. They were analysing the process. At many stages in their life they were suddenly faced with a crossroads. There were different options open to them and they changed their minds about where they were going. They sat down and rewrote the new plan.

All the way through their lives they were recording and commenting on their experiences, just like Thomas Edison in his laboratory. If he hadn't written down each and every experiment he would probably have repeated many experiments over and over again. Because he wrote down, for each one, what he was expecting to get and what he actually got and what the difference was between the two, this gave him some knowledge and some information to remember next time he did an experiment. If he got to experiment 200 he could go back to his notes and look at experiments four, five and six to see what he had learned at those stages of the process. That is precisely what these Harvard achievers did.

That, too, is why many people who achieve extraordinary things in their lives have the back-up evidence to write their autobiographies. They don't do it from memory, they do it from journals, and diaries and documents and processes. They have been recording their step-by-step journey through life – the dates, the times, the meetings, the people, the decisions they made, the places they were, the things that they did, the jobs they were doing.

That hooked me in. It is obviously not only a matter of writing it down, but writing it down seemed to me a funda-mental key, a fundamental discipline. I needed to start writing my plan of where I wanted to get to, and what the marker points would be on the way.

Let Go of Logic – Be Unreasonable

I was learning that the first step was that we must forget logic, forget the fact that goal-setting need not make any sense to the conscious mind. We must write goals down in the first person, present tense, positive frame – then we will be beginning to lie to our subconscious about what we have already experienced.

That meant that a goal must be *personal*. You can't set a goal for somebody else. It must be in the *present* tense. You have to install the goal subconsciously as if it has already occurred. You have to create the 'lie' for the tension to build. It must be *positive* and *emotional*. You have to think of what you want, and not what you want to avoid. You must record how you want the goal to make you feel.

Seeing Is Believing

The third step towards remaining purpose-full, in terms of goal-setting, is to install the process *emotionally* into your sub-conscious, not intellectually into your conscious mind. Just saying it, over and over again in a relentlessly positive affirmation, is not enough. The question now is how to put goals into your mind in the same way that Spielberg puts thoughts into your mind when you are watching his movies, or great writers put thoughts into your mind when you are reading their literature. How can you embed your goals at a very deep level in your consciousness?

The best method that I found was to start to create a very powerful, internal visualisation of what it was that I desired. If I wanted to teach, if I wanted to be immersed in this thinking and this body of knowledge, if I wanted to acquire wisdom in this field, and if I wanted to share this wisdom, then I needed to set up an organisation that could enable me to do that.

As I started to close my eyes and imagine what this might be I could see an organisation forming, a centre of excellence in all of these fields. I sat for a long while, and, instead of working out business plans and flow charts and spreadsheets, I just created a dream inside my head of what it would look like, what the company would look like, what I would be doing, what sort of platforms I would be speaking on, what sort of audiences I would be speaking to, what sort of books I might be writing, what sort of courses I might be teaching. I allowed myself to see it as if I was there. I started to jot down ideas and phrases on a piece of paper. One of the jottings was 'I want to create an Institute of Human Development in England.'

I suddenly discovered that for all of my life when I had dreamed my dreams, I had dreamed them way out there, in a field of vision way beyond the horizon. I was visualising Gilpin as a knight, bright-armoured on a glistening stallion, rescuing whichever damsel was of the moment, slaying whatever dragons he dreamed he was fighting. The pictures were separate from me, as if I was watching them on a movie screen. The images were clear enough, but the focus was on the horizon. They were a long way away. They were in the future.

Now, when I closed my eyes and I saw myself teaching, and I saw myself writing, and speaking to groups, it wasn't as if I was watching a movie. I had stepped into the movie. I was living it as though I was *there, now.* It was very different.

To experience the difference, take a moment now and imagine yourself sitting in a comfortable armchair, watching a video of an event you would like to happen. You can see the whole of yourself in it. The soundtrack is clear and you can hear yourself interacting with the other people there. Now do what you used to do as a child, play a game of make-believe. Imagine that you are standing up, and you are walking towards the television screen. As you walk towards it, it does what it can only do in a child's fantasy. It grows and grows and grows, until the picture appears all around you, and you are face to face with this other you, inside the dream. You take a step forward, and you are *in* the dream.

Dreaming Awake

You can no longer see you, because you *are* you. All you can see of you is your arms, and your legs and the rims of your spectacles: you are seeing it as if you are there. As you step into the experience, the emotional intensity that is attached to that dream increases a thousandfold. Your heart starts to beat faster, your hands start to sweat, you begin to feel as if this is already happening. You hear it in your own ears, you see it through your own eyes, you smell it, taste it. The most powerful thing you notice when you step into the dream is that you feel it internally, as you would feel it if it was happening to you now. It is like dreaming awake.

Dreaming awake, your subconscious mind experiences that

desired reality as if it *is* real. You can come out of the dream at any stage. When you come back out of the dream, back into the 'real' world, you realise that your present reality is a thousand miles away from that desired reality. Now you have two parts of your mind in disagreement with each other.

It is only at that moment – not when you are writing the goal, not when you are being purposeful about it – it is only when you step into that dream for real that your subconscious mind says, 'Now we have experienced this', and your conscious mind says, 'No, we haven't.' It is only now that you have the reality gap, and a tension and an energy and a dynamic in there that are going to give you the *potential* energy to move yourself on. You have created the dissonance that the subconscious mind is programmed to resolve, and it can only resolve it in one of two ways. It can either dream another, lesser dream, or it can make your present reality catch up with the dream. It *has* to resolve the dissonance for you to remain sane.

Mark Caine said, 'There are those who travel; and there are those who are going somewhere. They are different, and yet they are the same. The "success" has this over his rivals: he knows where he is going.' I would say, 'The success has this over his rivals: *he has already been where he is going.*'

I can imagine Roger Bannister (I don't know if this is true!) rehearsing his race over and over in his mind's eye, not as if he were watching a film, but as if he were actually there, feeling the burning, feeling the pain, going through the pain barrier. His hallucination, his dream, his fantasy would have been as real to him as the race itself, and he would have rehearsed that a thousand times.

Anecdotally it is reported that General Montgomery, when he was planning his campaigns against Rommel, would take this process one step further. Standing alone in his war room, he would view the maps of the battle scene through his own eyes, and he would make judgements about the manoeuvring of his troops, and his tactics. He would then walk to the other side of the map board and adopt the physiology of Rommel, standing as Rommel stood, breathing as Rommel breathed, looking at the whole process through Rommel's eyes, as if he *were* Rommel. He would enter into a fantasy state as Rommel, and respond as Rommel. Then he would go back to his original place and, Montgomery once again, he would see how Rommel was likely to respond to his moves, so he could respond in his turn.

Andrew Carnegie, the Scottish-born American industrialist and philanthropist who amassed a fortune in the steel industry, when tackling a difficult decision with a group of people, would say, 'Excuse me, gentlemen, for one moment. I will go and consult with my Board.' He would step into a private room and he would sit alone at a table, close his eyes, and imagine he was there, in a room with his closest advisers. He would ask each of them in turn what they would do, and what their advice was. He held that meeting inside his imagination, as if it were real. He would gather the advice and the opinions, and all the resources he needed from this meeting, then make a decision based on that. He would open his eyes, return to the 'real' meeting, and say, 'My Board and I have decided the following . . .'

That is how you create the desired reality, how you actually live it as if it is real. That is the conditioning process by which you explore huge unfathomed depths, vaguely apprehended aspects of your mind. You access parts of your subconscious that no one fully understands. Though you don't understand its full power you can still begin to access it so that the pursuit of your goals is not just a conscious, logical, rational, procedural process. It is something that is drawing down and tapping into the full power of your mind.

Those who live their dreams are able to access a different part of their consciousness, a different part of their psychology, to attain their goals.

Unlocking Resources

I realised that, if I wanted to set up an Institute of Human Development, a centre of excellence in the field of human potential, all the expertise I needed already existed, all the academic research I needed already existed. All the money I would need already existed, all the people that I needed to make it happen were already there. The time it was going to take was already available. I probably had the qualities that were required to make it happen. Everything was sitting there, somewhere in the world. It wasn't that the things I needed didn't exist. I didn't have to create them or invent them. My job was to *find* them.

By conditioning my subconscious with visualisation I was opening up a part of my brain called the *reticular activating cortex,* which is a fibrous network of cells operating like a set of antennae. When you take a brand-new car on the road for the first time it is the reticular activating cortex that ensures that you immediately see all the cars that match the one you have just bought. Those cars were out there all the time before, but you just didn't notice them. Now they have become significant to you.

It is this part of your brain that works when you need a new washing machine, or a computer, or something you have never had before and you have no idea where to look for it. You open a newspaper and there it is, with a sale price attached to it. You would have seen the advertisement in the paper anyway, but you would never have noticed it until it became significant to you.

It is this part of your brain that you use when something is on the tip of your tongue, or you have just seen someone whose name you can't recall, or you're trying to remember what it was that you promised not to forget. Your reticular activating system is awake, it has been asked a question, and its job is to seek out the answer.

It is this part of your brain that is alert when you have

extraordinary 'coincidences'. For instance, you feel there is a story you need to illustrate a point you are making in a report, or a speech or an article. You have been sitting staring at a blank piece of paper or computer screen and nothing has come. You wander aimlessly round the room and idly pick up a book, or a magazine, and there is the quote you wanted, there is the idea you needed, there is the thought that would just get you under way.

It is these coincidences in our lives that are created by us being ready, and being open to them. The reticular activating cortex filters out 99.9 per cent of the millions of pieces of information presented to us through our senses every second. Most of it is irrelevant at any one moment, but when we make the decision that something is significant and relevant, suddenly we know where to look. I could talk to someone for hours without being aware of my year-planner on the wall, but if I need to look for a date, I know precisely where to look.

In *The Doors of Perception*, Aldous Huxley wrote that experience 'has to be funnelled through the reducing valves of the brain and nervous system. What comes out the other end is a measly trickle of the kind of consciousness which will help us to stay alive on the surface of this particular planet.'

Your reticular activating cortex filters out most of the things you don't need, and only allows through the things that are significant to you. If you set your goals in this way, if you write them in the first person, present tense, positive frame, if you live them as though they already exist and have already happened, then, when you get out there in the 'real' world, you spot the people, the money, the technology, the resources and the time that you need to make them happen. You may have been driving past them, metaphorically, on the motorway, but now Jaguars or BMWs or red MGs are significant to you, and you spot every one of those, but you don't register the thousands of other cars that go past.

Planting the Seeds

At this moment in the embryonic history of the Institute of Human Development, I knew that if it was going to become real, if I was going to be standing on the platforms that I was standing on in my dreams, if I was going to be writing the books, including this book, that I was writing in my dreams, then I needed to raise significant research and development funding and capital to make this happen. I started to write down, in my goal-setting process, some of the resources I might need, and some of the people that I might need.

One of the resources I identified, one of the people I felt might be interested, and might be able to help, was the new Chief Executive of Kent TEC. He was a man about whom I knew very little, except his reputation for being deeply committed to providing the resources for other people to become excellent, and his reputation for making things happen. He had just been appointed when I first heard his name, Malcolm Allan. I wrote the name 'Malcolm Allan' in what I call my 'resource list' in my Filofax.

I could have written to him: 'Dear Mr Allan, You won't know me. I want to do this. I'd like some money from you, please. Thank you very much.'

I would have received from him one of the countless letters I have received in my career: 'Dear Mr Gilpin, What an interesting idea. It sounds absolutely delightful. We wish you the very best fortune with it. Unfortunately we are in no position at the moment to invest in this sort of scheme. Regretfully . . .' Like many people, I have files and files of those sorts of letters from randomly thought-out projects written to randomly identified resources.

'This time,' I thought, 'I'm going to do it differently. This time I'm going to imagine that we are meeting. I'm going to imagine that we are having a conversation about providing people with the tools that they need to become excellent, to

cope in an ever-changing society, to move away from the lack
of advantage that they had in their childhood and the lack of
good fortune they have had so far in their business career, the
tools that they need to move on to better things and to new
horizons.' I imagined that conversation, and I left it at that.

I was planting the seeds in my subconscious, and leaving
them alone to grow.

A number of weeks later, perhaps eight or ten weeks, I was
at a dinner held by the Institute of Directors at Chilham Castle,
in Kent. It just so happened that a couple of associates of mine
were manipulating the seating plan at the last minute to put me
next to someone who wanted to persuade me to come on to the
Board of the local Education Business Partnership.

I introduced myself to the person on my right, and the
people around me. As it happened there was a gap directly
opposite me. A while later a man arrived and I stretched out my
hand and said, 'Good evening, good to meet you. I am Adrian
Gilpin . . .'

'Hello,' he said, 'I'm Malcolm Allan, Chief Executive of
Kent TEC.'

I said, 'Am I pleased to meet you!'

He looked very surprised. 'Good Heavens, why?'

'I have a feeling you and I may be able to do business together. I have a feeling you may be interested in some of the
things we are developing. I know you are new at the TEC, I
know that you probably haven't had time to get your feet under
the table yet, but when you have I'd love to have a chance to
meet with you.'

Malcolm, being a very wise man, said to me, 'Well, before
you tell me what your proposal is, why don't I tell you what my
first thoughts are about the strategy for Kent TEC?'

He spent much of the next three hours telling us that what
he was interested in doing was building the self-esteem of
learners, teaching people how to learn, giving them the tools

for excellence to move themselves from modest success to peak performance . . . We were having the conversation that I had already had.

That was an eerie experience for me, then. More and more now I find that if I am living my goals at the deep level of my subconscious, then I am opening up my reticular activating cortex to spot all of those resources that already exist. I am not creating them, I am simply noticing them. Before, Malcolm and I might have shaken hands, 'How nice to meet you', and we would have had small talk for the rest of the evening.

I have learned that it is critical to identify the resources you are going to need, and not just write them down on a piece of paper. We are so used, in business, to writing our business plans saying we are going to need this money, these people, this sort of warehouse, this sort of office space, this sort of technology. We write down a list to which we have no emotional attachment. All the time we are writing the list we may well be saying in the back of our minds, 'Oh, yes, in your dreams. Where are we going to get all this from?' There is a limiting belief undermining those ideas, and the exercise becomes fruitless.

I was doing it differently. I constructed the goal, I dreamed the dream. Now I was gathering the resources to make those dreams come true; gathering them with the power of my subconscious as well as my conscious mind. My conscious mind was telling me what we needed, and my subconscious mind was going out there to find it.

People who achieve extraordinary things have learned how to bring the conscious and subconscious minds into rapport with each other. As these two parts of your mind come to-gether, you will discover whether you believe in your goal or not. You will get a warm and excited feeling inside, a sense of knowing that this is right. If things are not right, you will feel it too – a churning stomach which says oh-oh, there's something wrong. It is that in-side information, that *in-sight* that is coming from the gut, that tells you, 'Pay attention. There's something not right. There's something missing.'

It was at this stage in the project that I found myself with my stomach churning, thinking on the one hand, 'Boy, oh boy, this stuff *works*. What if I, literally, could have anything I wanted, simply by dreaming it in this way?'; and on the other hand, ' Do I believe that I can do this? Do I believe I can have this?'

There were warning signals coming from inside me. I asked myself, 'What does this outcome mean for me?' It would mean that I was creating from scratch, from my own imagination, from my own creativity, a centre of excellence in a field that fascinated me. I was doing this on my own. For the first time in my life this was an entrepreneurial venture, a vocational venture, that wasn't coming from somebody else. I'd always been very good at making projects happen for other people. Here was something where I was now in the lead.

If I could have that, would I take it? The simple answer was yes, I would. There was another reason.

Magic

All through my life I had been fascinated by magic, by change, by the processes of taking something and transforming it into another form. As a child I had been fascinated by sleight of hand and conjuring, and now I was becoming fascinated by sleight of mouth, by the words and the language of influence and persuasion; fascinated by the thought of taking people who were in a place of pain and moving them to a place of comfort, taking people from a place where they didn't believe in themselves to a place where they could believe in their uniqueness.

It was exactly the same as the magician putting somebody in a box. When he opens the box, there is somebody else. The conjuring tricks that had enthralled me as a child were all about getting people to see something from a different perspective, about the truth being different from what the audience thought they saw. The stories I loved as a teenager were about the process of transformation, of people appearing to be one thing and being revealed as another, or people discovering who they really were. The magic and the wizardry of personal change is about giving people the opportunity to see things from a different perspective, too, so that they can discover that they are more than they think they have become.

So, not only was it appropriate to my sense of self, but it seemed to me that at last I had found a job that did what was at the heart of me. Now I could begin.

13: INTO THE KNOWN

Taking a new step, uttering a new word, is what people fear most.

FYODOR DOSTOEVSKY

The next step was to take action.

The one fundamental step that is missing from so many, if not all, the goal-setting, strategic-planning models that I have ever seen, whether they are business-planning, objective-setting, personal goal-setting or positive affirmations, is the step that says, 'What are you going to do *now* to take action? What is the next step?'

The next step for me was incorporating an organisation called the Institute of Human Development. That was what I had written in my goal-setting jottings, that is what I had decided to do.

I picked up the phone to speak to my lawyer. I said, 'I want to set up a company to be called the Institute of Human Development.'

He said, 'You can't do that.'

'Why not?'

'There are a handful of business names that are restricted by government in the UK, and one of them happens to be "institute".'

'What do I have to do to become an institute?'

'You wouldn't be able to, Adrian. Choose another name.'

'I don't intend to choose another name. I have decided that I'm going to set up the Institute of Human Development. Would you, please, send me all the documentation I need, so that I know what I have to do to set up an institute?'

A hundredweight of paper arrived. The Department of Trade and Industry set up some very daunting obstacles and objections – hoops we had to jump through before I could set up my business. I said to myself, 'Why get fixed on a name? I could call it anything – the Association of Human Development, Peak Performance Coaching Inc., anything.'

But, no. In my dream I had set up the Institute of Human Development. Was I about to stumble at the first hurdle? Was I about to allow the dream to slip one step closer to present reality? I didn't know (I still don't) why the word Institute came to mind. Perhaps it was my pomposity. Whatever the reason, 'Institute' was the word I had written down in my goal-setting process, so that is what it would be.

I went through the process with the DTI. I gathered the information, I gathered the resources, I gathered the approval from the many-headed government bodies. I proved the need, I proved that nobody else was covering the same ground. I jumped through every hoop.

In January we were finally granted Institute status, as a Private Limited Company in receipt of public-sector funding, through the Kent Training and Enterprise Council.

The next step was to put dates in the diary. If I was going to be delivering programmes, then they had to be real. They had to be on the time line. They had to be in the diary. I set dates. I invited hundreds of local business people to short briefings to hear all about our seminars.

At that stage I hadn't written the seminars and I hadn't written the briefings. I had written the invitations, though, and I had put them in the post. Now I was committed.

I had about six months to prepare. The time approached, and the time approached. Still there was nothing written. The research was continuing. The books were being read. The tapes were being listened to. The seminars were being attended. Nothing was on paper.

With about three weeks to go I decided I needed to write something. I wrote outlines to three core programmes, *Universal Laws of Achievement*, *Pathways to Personal Effectiveness* and *Building the Vision and Making It Happen*. I decided that our core curriculum was going to be three seminar programmes, each three days long. I wrote a two-hour briefing about each, describing what they would enable you to do, and giving some facilitated examples of what would happen in the full programmes.

When I put out those invitations I was expecting to run six days of briefings across two different venues in Kent. I had chosen two beautiful private country houses, and I expected to attract ten to twelve people to each one. As it turned out, something like two hundred and forty people came along. Chief executives and senior managers from Kent's largest businesses and public-sector organisations had responded to their invitations.

Suddenly, there I was at my first briefing, standing in front of an audience talking about the things I had been doing over the last few years, talking about the strategies I had been learning, and talking with passion. I didn't realise until it was all over that I had spoken without a single note in my hand.

I handed out feedback forms, and I received extraordinarily complimentary responses. There was a huge level of interest. Within days we had people booking places for the full curriculum and paying money!

I still hadn't written the seminars.

Between the briefings in July and the first programme in September I wrote nine days of teaching. I wrote the course notes, wrote the participants' manuals, wrote my own notes. I had to pull in the anecdotes, choose the examples. I had to test and retest it, write it and rewrite it, edit material out and edit material back in.

So, that is what I did. I have never worked harder in my life.

I had never experienced so much passion and excitement and terror together.

I ran the first programme on schedule in September, to what can be described as a kind of collective hysteria from the twelve participants, in terms of the impact I was having on their thinking, and the way they were able to apply the strategies in their businesses and their homes. Before the cycle was complete their business partners, and their spouses, and their friends and associates were booking on to the next series, for which I hadn't even set dates. I felt enormously privileged to have been given this chance and to have found people who wanted to embark on their own journeys with me as a guide. The experience was exciting, scary and very humbling.

The Institute was up and running.

I had dreamed the dream. I had come back to 'reality' and written down what I had dreamed. I had found that as you start the dreaming process, the dream takes over. Crucially, what takes the dream out of the dream, and makes it live in the present reality, is your *ability to take action*. The words of one of J. R. R. Tolkien's characters that I had read many years before came back to me, 'It's the job that's never started as takes longest to finish.' I had started.

Beyond the Dragon

> *Some who are called to the adventure choose to go,*
> *others may wrestle for years with fearfulness and*
> *denial before they are able to transcend that fear. We*
> *tend to deny our destiny because of our insecurity,*
> *our dread of ostracism, and our anxiety and our lack*
> *of courage to risk what we have.*
>
> JOSEPH JAWORSKI

I felt I was still a long way from transcending the fear that Jaworski writes about. I am not sure that I have transcended that fear yet. I am not yet convinced that I will transcend that fear entirely and for ever. What I do know is that a moment comes when you face it, and you name it, and continue to go forward, regardless.

Courage, it seems, doesn't come from an ability to suppress the fear. I do not believe that by 'transcend' Jaworski means 'rise above' the fear – become fear-less. By 'transcend' I believe he means 'pass beyond'. Courage is the willingness to face the fear dragon and not turn back.

In the title of her book, *Feel the Fear and Do It Anyway*, Susan Jeffries describes my experience at this moment on my journey. Often, still, as I take a step forward, as I think of the next phase of development, of the next project, of the task of writing a book like this, the fear and the anxiety are palpable – I can taste them and breathe them in but they no longer stop me taking the necessary action.

An image that remains constantly in my mind is that of the climber or mountaineer. As you learn to deal with this anxiety and fear you simply allow yourself to climb a steeper hill, or a higher mountain range. The fear becomes greater, not less, the danger becomes greater, not less, the courage that is needed becomes more, not less, but the process becomes more addictive, more stimulating and more rewarding.

As you embark on your new journeys, as you climb your higher hills, as you risk more with each step you see views and landscapes that fewer and fewer and fewer people have seen.

Although I cannot imagine myself climbing to the top of Everest literally, I can begin to imagine what it is like for someone who has stood on top of that mountain and looked down at a sight that he or she has shared with only a handful of other human beings. That is a powerful metaphor for me.

As I take the steps up my particular hills and mountains, in my particular area of work, I have the opportunity to view things that relatively few other human beings will view. That is what keeps me going on. What enables me to deal with the anxiety and the fear is that the rewards of courage are unimaginable.

All the teachers and masters mentioned in this book are climbing their own mountains, in their own way. They are all dealing with their own anxieties, their own fears, in their own way. In doing so they gain rewards that are unimaginable to the rest of humanity. That is what makes them special. That is what makes them unstoppable.

14: DREAM TEAMS

Follow then the shining ones, the wise, the awakened,
the loving, for they know how to work and forbear.

THE BUDDHA

I had crossed the threshold. I had climbed past the fear dragon. I had stepped forward and accepted responsibility and a commitment to a new standard of thinking, and a new standard of expectation for myself. I had set new targets for my achievements. As a result, I knew I was now going to encounter greater hurdles than I had ever encountered before, not lesser ones.

To overcome these I was now equipping myself with new thinking skills and attitudinal skills. I had identified and I was now testing my new beliefs and values. I had acquired a fresh sense of self and was discovering a sense of purpose. Now I needed someone to keep me on track, to keep me on my chosen pathway.

Not only from my teachers and the people that I read and those people that I imagine as my mentors, but also from the real people that I meet, I have built, and I keep building, the team I need to help me forward on my quest. I am not alone. Around me I have a team. I call it my dream team.

The dream team keeps me focused, asks the questions to keep my mind on track: 'What do you want? What will you get from this? How will this serve your current purpose? What direction are you now heading in? What will be the consequences of this? What will be the outcomes of that decision?'

Response-ability

Now I knew that not only was it possible to choose my own pathway and take command of my journey, but I was beginning to do that. This alone enhanced, and resonated through, all the things that were important to me: my values, the things I believed I was capable of achieving, who I was starting to discover I was, perhaps even what my purpose might be, and what legacy I would be able to leave behind.

With each step on my journey, new colours, new shapes, new sketches were forming on my previously blank canvas. A landscape was beginning to develop. Growing within me was the sense of a genuine power to determine my own direction and my own destiny. I was taking command of my own actions and my own responses to the challenges that I was encountering, and the challenges that I would continue to encounter.

With this came an overwhelming sense of personal responsibility for everything that was happening. I had started to realise that every circumstance I had found myself in, throughout my entire life, had been a product of my own thinking. I had made that major breakthrough in coming to terms with being the cause of all the changes in my life, being 'at cause', not 'at effect', being the agent of events, not the victim.

This responsibility was daunting. Accepting that you are at the cause of everything that happens in your life is not an easy decision to take. However other people react to me, whatever happens to my projects, to my successes, to my failures is *not* caused by the world, the economy, the government, my wife, my children, my colleagues or the devious manipulation of other people. It is the product of my own thinking.

Ultimately I am going to move relentlessly in the direction of my thoughts.

This is why some people who contract terminal disease and are given three months to live refuse to think in that way, and, like Robert Dilts' mother, get themselves thirteen years. It is why some people who find themselves confined to a wheelchair will not accept it as fact when somebody tells them, 'You can't climb a mountain.' They decide to think in a different way, and their thinking is so powerfully focused that it enables them to achieve those outcomes, however bizarre and absurd they seem to the rest of us.

Now I was beginning to take responsibility for my life I went back to the teaching of someone who was becoming more and more influential in my life, a man called Stephen Covey. One of the most powerful insights that I have had from Stephen Covey's work is his simple definition of the word 'responsibility'.

Responsibility is not about taking the blame, responsibility is not about taking the credit. Responsibility is about having the ability to respond. It is not 'respons-ibility', Covey says, it is *response-ability*, the ability to respond to whatever happens to you externally.

When you take that responsibility to become what Covey calls *response-able*, you let go of all the excuses, all the crutches that have enabled you to blame the world or other people for your challenges, or handicaps. You know that the world is not focused primarily on serving you. You know that things will happen in the world that are good, that are average, and that are bad. It is not what happens to you that makes any difference to your destiny, it is how you choose to *respond* to what happens to you that makes the difference to your destiny.

The same thing can happen to six of us in a project. Two of us will respond well, two of us will not respond, and two of us will respond badly. It is not the external input that makes any difference, it is how we respond to it.

Though I have now taken the decision to be response-able I still wish I was able to live it twenty-four hours a day, seven days a week. I don't, but I am aware, instantly, when the old voice returns to find a reason or a cause for my situation and my circumstance that isn't anything to do with me. I hear that voice: I no longer like the sound of that voice. I am no longer prepared to let that voice dictate the terms.

Unstoppable People

The question I faced now was, did I have the qualities and character that would be needed to sustain me on this pathway for the rest of my life? The simple answer was, I didn't know. I knew for certain that I couldn't do this alone.

I looked back at the stories of the great achievers that I had been encountering over the past five years. Whether it was the story of Nelson Mandela's *Long Walk to Freedom*; whether it was the story of Kathy Buckley's long walk through cancer, and rape, and abuse; whether it was the story of Tony Robbins' journey from his job as a janitor to his rôle as one of the most powerful and inspiring communicators in America; whether it was the story of Lee Van Vu and his journey from the escape from Saigon to forging a new life for himself in America; whether it was Joseph Jaworski, Charles Dunstone or Richard Branson – what was clear to me was that *these people had become unstoppable people.*

I look at all these people, and they all seem to have more than one thing in common. Yes, they have all faced the fear dragon; yes, they have all discovered something inside themselves that was inherently powerful; but all the ones I had talked to, all the ones I had read about, all the ones who were prepared to share their stories in detail, revealed one crucial thing to me. That was their commitment to finding teachers and mentors, gurus and guides, who kept them on track.

Dream Teams

For me, the people that had become part of my life over the past five years were becoming my dream team. Many of them I had never met, some of them I had only listened to on platforms, some of them I had only encountered through their writing. Some of them I had sat and worked and shared out my experiences with.

At the same time I was gathering around me people like myself, who were on the same journey. Some of them had started after me. Some of them had been on the journey for years. Gradually we were forming a network of people who knew that the future of our businesses, our communities, our societies, even our globe was in the hands of people who were acquiring a new way of thinking.

I resolved to surround myself with a number of dream teams. My most intimate team would consist of one, two or three close mentors: my coaches, my teachers, people I could turn to when I was struggling, unsure, uncertain, the same people that I hoped would come to me when they needed that kind of support. A wider dream team would include the teachers that I met, and the teachers that I listened to on a regular basis, the people whose seminars I attended, the people whose books I read.

In the Out-field

In an outer-circle dream team would be the people that I had not met, and was unlikely to meet, but whose stories, writings and reputations were an inspiration and a motivation and a reminder to me, on a daily basis, of what it is to be, in Covey's word, response-able. I would be surrounded by their books. I would be surrounded by reminders of the heart and the spirit and the thinking of people like Mahatma Gandhi, whose story had taught me so much about the power of a simple, single focus; and taught me so much about internal honesty or integrity or congruence.

There is a great story about Gandhi that I heard many years ago.

One day, when Gandhi was meeting with the people, he was approached by a woman who said, 'I have travelled many miles with my son to meet you. You are the only person of whom my son is in awe and whom my son respects. I want you to tell him to stop eating so much sugar. You can see how overweight he is, how unhealthy he is becoming. I have told him; his father has told him; his friends have told him. If you tell him, he will listen and he will stop.'

Gandhi replied, 'Go away. Come back in three weeks' time.'

The woman protested, 'We have travelled so long. It is so far to our home. It is impossible for us to go all the way back home and return within three weeks.'

Gandhi said, 'Please. Take your son away. Come back in three weeks' time.'

She went away, dismayed. Three weeks later they returned. They queued for half a day to speak to Gandhi. When, eventually, they reached him she reminded him of their conversation three weeks before. 'We have waited for many hours to ask again that you may speak to my son. If you tell him to stop eating so much sugar he will do so. Before, you told me to go away and come back in three weeks. Now I am here again with my son.'

Gandhi turned to the boy. 'If you will listen to me, stop eating sugar. It is bad for you. It is unhealthy.'

The woman looked at him and said, 'Please tell me, why wouldn't you say this to him three weeks ago? It is such a simple thing to say.'

Gandhi returned her look. With a smile he said, 'Three weeks ago I was eating sugar.'

Then there was Kathy Buckley, telling us the story of her journey through deafness and cancer, her journey through abuse, rejection and her crippling spine injury. She stood on a platform and twelve hundred people laughed until they wept with the pain of their laughter. In a heartbeat she turned their tears of joy into tears of sadness as she drew us into the deep and dark tragedy of her story. Just as we felt we could stand the tragedy no longer, she used a phrase or a gesture that had us laughing again until we ached all over. In an instant she took us down again to the depths of the pain that she, and others like her, had suffered. She led her audience from one emotional extreme to another.

She taught me the phenomenal power of personal command. By that I do not mean the emotional control that so many of us have grown used to, the ability to ignore what is going on inside us, to reject the emotional responses and silence them with drink or drugs, or promiscuity or procrastination, or anger or frustration or aggression. I mean allowing yourself to be willing to experience the depths of despair, honestly and passionately in front of other people, and at the same time allowing yourself to experience a joy and an ecstasy and a passion that few people enjoy in their lifetime.

Lee Van Vu taught me that it is not what you have in terms of money, language, resources or support that makes the blindest bit of difference to where you will end up in your life, but it is what you do with those resources and how you respond to the challenges that you will face.

Deepak Chopra enabled me to believe that at a very deep spiritual level we are co-creators of our own experience in this world; that as we think, so we become; as we think, so we achieve. With every thought, and with every word that we use in the privacy of our minds or in our communications with other people, we are creating a version of reality that, to all intents and purposes, is the one that we will experience.

Nelson Mandela, Victor Frankl, Terry Waite and John McCarthy explain, each in his own unique and powerful way, that when you are imprisoned for what may be a lifetime, even if it is in a cell twelve feet square like Captain Gerald Coffey's during the Vietnam War, the one thing 'they', your captors, cannot take away from you is your freedom. Aleksandr Solzhenitsyn explores the same themes in his novel *One Day in the Life of Ivan Denisovich*. To me, this was a bizarre concept, until I understood that what they meant by this was that the one thing that 'they' cannot take away from us is our *freedom to decide what each experience means.*

> *You only have power over people so long as you don't take everything away from them. But when you've robbed a man of everything he's no longer in your power – he's free again.*
> ALEKSANDR SOLZHENITSYN, BOBYNIN, IN *THE FIRST CIRCLE*

In his book about his experience of Auschwitz, *Man's Search for Meaning*, Victor Frankl tells how he watched people's spirits die a long time before their bodies. Those were the people who had attached to their terrible experiences meaning such as 'mankind is evil', or 'I must have sinned', or 'there is no God'. Victor Frankl attached a meaning, which was that he was there for a reason and a purpose, and that reason was clear to him. He was there to survive, and to make the world see what had happened, and to make sure that it never happened again. The spirit that stayed alive in him was his freedom to choose his reason for being in that situation.

The lesson is the same from Mandela, and from the hostages: 'The one thing they cannot take from us is our freedom to decide what this means.'

The In-field

Here, perhaps, it is less appropriate to mention the members of the inner circles of the dream teams by name. They are the people that I am bringing into my inner circle of advisers to the Institute of Human Development. They are people who are, first and foremost, my friends, some of whom will become my professional colleagues. They are the people who over the last five years of my life have simply, out of love and friendship, been willing to sit, sometimes for hours or for days on end, prompting, asking me questions, and keeping me focused. They nurture my belief in the project, in myself, and in the team we are becoming. They keep me focused on the value of teaching people how to take command of their own lives, their relationships, their careers.

One thing that doesn't come through from a short summary, like this book, is the extraordinary challenges, difficulties, delays and financial demands that we have encountered during the years of setting up the Institute of Human Development. Each one of those has sometimes seemed insurmountable, but only for a moment, only while the old voices are murmuring. My coaches and my teachers and my mentors remind me that I have a new voice, a less practised one, a less familiar one, but a voice that asks the questions, 'Why?' 'What do you want? Why do you want it?' 'What is the reason for this?' 'What is the purpose?'

These questions are at the heart of the purpose of being a coach or a mentor, a guide or a teacher or a guru.

Pavarotti doesn't have a better opera singer to coach him. Torvill and Dean don't have better ice dancers to coach them. Pete Sampras has a fitness trainer, Todd Snyder, to keep him focused on peak condition. Until recently he had a team of coaches, one for footwork, one for serve, one for forehand technique. Now he works with world-class coach, Paul Annacone, whose task is to draw out of Sampras his championship brilliance. Annacone is not a better tennis-player than Sampras; that is not his rôle. Sir John Harvey-Jones would find it difficult to find more skilful business administrators to coach him. Yet these masters still choose to work with mentors and coaches who can coax out of them their own unique qualities and excellence. They find people who can keep them to the standards they have set for themselves; remind them of their purpose and of who they are; remind them of what they have done right; remind them of what they want to achieve and have not achieved yet. That is the task of the coach and the mentor.

Often, in my seminars, I remind my audience of the opening title sequences of a programme that ran for many years on television. It was called *Kung Fu* and featured David Carradine in the rôle of Little Grasshopper. Each episode started with David Carradine sitting in front of his guru, or master. He would, invariably, present a problem or ask his master a question about how to achieve something. His master, invariably, answered in what, to Little Grasshopper and the audience, was an incoherent riddle. Little Grasshopper would wander away with that riddle in his mind, but still with no clarity as to what his master meant, or intended. Eventually, by living his life with that riddle endlessly running in his mind, he would discover its power and value, and its answer.

It seems to me that what I have learned from the people who have been willing to give me their time and their energy and their excellence, is that these are people who ask me questions that at first I do not fully understand. They guide me and prompt me. They almost never give me advice.

'Advice,' wrote the Earl of Chesterfield to his son, 'is seldom welcome; and those who want it the most always like it the least.'

His son probably wanted to answer in the words Thoreau wrote a hundred years or so later: 'I have lived some thirty years on this planet, and I have yet to hear the first syllable of valuable . . . advice from my seniors.'

So, if you want to help me, don't give me the right advice.

Ask me the right questions.

15: THE COACH

You can drop your personal history right now. Just drop it . . . What you need is a teacher to teach you that you have immeasurable power within you.

DR WAYNE DYER

*I*t has become clearer and clearer to me that I am the only one who has the answers to my life's questions. I am the only one with the map of my life's path, and the key to my life's destiny. My personality is extremely unlikely to be willing to accept straightforward, blatant advice or recommendations from other people. Only *I* have the answers to what I want to achieve; only *I* have the answers to how I am going to achieve that.

The gift I have been given by my mentors is the discovery that they can help me find those answers, by listening, prompting, asking me questions, setting me riddles that I must solve for myself. If there is anything that I try to focus on all the way through my own teaching and my own seminars it is this – the ability to ask just the right question, in just the right way, at just the right time for someone to discover that the answer lay within them all the way along.

The Power of Coaching

Each of the unstoppable people that I encounter has discovered that dormant and silent within each of us are the answers to so many challenges, problems, and confusions. Questions are the keys that unlock potential. Potential is what lies way beyond what you currently imagine yourself to be capable of. All you need is to find the right coach, the right teacher, the right mentor, whose focus and whose precision with questions help you unlock the windows of your in-sight and open the doorways to your own solutions.

The Power of Questions

If I am coaching you alone, or if I am working with two hundred people in an audience, I can easily tell you *about* these things. I can interest you intellectually. On the other hand I can set you a riddle or ask you a question which makes something happen inside your mind that becomes a deep and penetrating in-sight. That moment of self-discovery, of awakening, of satori, can only happen if the answer is drawn out of you, rather than fed into you by someone else.

Right back at the beginning, I learned with the consultant who asked me, 'Adrian, what do you *want?*'; then with Tony Robbins, who asked in a more complex way, 'Adrian, if you knew you could not possibly fail, what would you do . . . what do you really *want?*'; then from Stephen Covey who asked, 'Are you starting with the end in mind?', that the secret lies with people who have the ability to ask us the right questions, rather than simply teach us; to wake us up to the possibilities, rather than impose on us their solutions; to help us to find our own pathways, rather than simply put into us *their* map of the world.

My frustration with consultancy was that we listened to the client talk about his business. We repeated it back to the client. We told him all the things that he had been teaching us about his business, put our spin on it, and said, 'If we were you, this is what we would do.'

Consultancy projects are rarely implemented with full commitment, vigour and passion when they are imposed in that way by an external consultant. Where external consultants have extraordinary power is when they know how to ask generative questions which shift your focus away from the problems and towards solutions. Generative questions shift your thinking away from what is going wrong to what you want to go right; from the things you don't know yet, to the things you want to discover; from the cost of investing, to the benefits that will be reaped. Generative questions shift you away from what your competition did last year to what you want to do this year: shift you away from what you think is possible based upon last year's results, to what you want to be possible, based upon the question, 'If you knew you couldn't possibly fail, what would you do now?'

That constant refocusing, shifting of your focus away from what is wrong with your personal relationships and your marriage, to what magic you have experienced in it; shifting your children's thinking away from all of the things they think they *can't* do, to all of the things they have discovered that they *can do* and that they want to do, can, in my experience, only be done by asking the right questions, in the right way, at the right time.

Unleashing Potential

Almost invariably you don't achieve quantum shifts by telling somebody the facts about the world. You may be right, but you're only right about *your* world. It may be the right solution for you, but that doesn't mean that it is the right solution for them. If it is the right solution for them, they need to be coaxed towards it and they need to be able to find it on their own. They know the right answers; it is up to you to ask the right questions.

As a stage director, Francesca *could* dictate what to do and how to do it. She *could* expect her actors to be marionettes to her puppet-master. Or, and this is how she does it, she could gently coax, prompt, provoke and challenge so that their inner talent is unleashed and flows in torrents on to the stage. What happens in these moments is magical: the artist accesses a power that he or she could only dream of and a *character* grows in place of a *performance*. I remember this whenever I can when

I am working with business people. I could try to get a team to do it my way and achieve everything that I am capable of; or I can explore the passions, talents, insights and genius of a team and achieve more than any of us could have dreamed of. Perhaps this stems from an innate belief that on my own I can achieve only so much; others can always get more out of me than I can find on my own. I am beginning to know that this is generally true of people.

The key is to allow people the freedom to discover for themselves, and then *leave them with that discovery*. Francesca does not say to her actors, 'Well, actually, that was *my* idea.' If Francesca's intention is to get to the vision that she has in mind, she can do it by planting the seeds, asking the questions. When her cast comes up with an idea whose first seed she has planted hours or days before Francesca says, 'That's brilliant!' *because what they have done with it is.* Francesca's purpose is to get a result on the stage, not get the credit for every moment of genius the show produces. My purpose in a coaching programme is to get *you* to discover your own extraordinary power. My rôle should not be overt. Though your coach, mentor, guide, teacher can often stand firm and challenge you, often, he will be transparent, like a wizard whose spell touches you silently and invisibly.

I have learned a technique to get myself quickly into that silent listening state during a workshop or seminar, when someone asks a question that matters deeply to them. Often this comes right in the middle of a particularly passionate and exciting train of thought. I have to switch modes in an instant from 'putting out' to 'finding out'. I step quickly to take a sip of water from my glass. I hold it in a certain way that I copied from one of my greatest teachers, Ian McDermott of International Teaching Seminars. Ian is one of the great masters of silent listening – that space where you listen without judgement, observing nothing consciously and everything subconsciously so that when you respond you do so spontaneously and with a perfect insight. As I copy his stance and style just for a moment, I am transported back into his seminar rooms and into my version of what I believe is his silent listening state. Ian's guidance which once was real and tangible is now invisible and magical – touching me in moments when it is most needed.

The Method

> *To know how to suggest is the great art of teaching.*
> *To attain it we must be able to guess what will*
> *interest; we must learn to read the childish soul as we*
> *might a piece of music. Then, by simply changing the*
> *key, we keep up the attraction and vary the song.*
> HENRI-FRÉDÉRIC AMIEL

Wise questioning unleashes thinking processes which open up a world of possibilities that the conscious mind will not find on its own. Being a great questioner is part of my sense of self that I value. The same skills are there for you to learn.

I first discovered the power of questioning reading about the Socratic method of inquiry. Socrates was described in 399 BC as being (among other things) 'a curious person, searching into things under the earth and above the heaven; and making the worse appear the better cause, and teaching all this to others'. The process he developed for his search was to start discussions among the brightest young men in Athens by questioning, as if he were much stupider than they were, their opinions on apparently ordinary, everyday things that everybody thought they knew all about. The process usually revealed that the young men hadn't really even started to think through the most basic things, or tried to define the things that were really important to them. Socrates seems to have stopped there. It was the people who came after him that started to use his methods to discover answers to the vital questions about ourselves and what we know and believe.

I began to learn this process by studying the work of Chomsky, and those same concepts in practical application by the great therapists like Milton Erickson and Virginia Satir, and the brilliant questioning processes that they developed to get inside the map of the world that was being presented to them by their patients. Their method was to get inside that map and not to come out with any presupposition as to what this person needed to heal them. They tried to get the healing process drawn out of the individual so that individuals started to understand their own map of the world and how it was limiting them. Just as Socrates had, they developed their own processes of precision questioning to expose alternative, broader visions of possibility.

Power Questions
Some of the most powerful tools to come out of the field of psychology known as Neuro-Linguistic Programming are the questioning models known as the 'Milton Model' and the 'Meta Model'. These are worth an investment of time to study.

The Milton Model has been built around Milton Erickson's questioning skills. Erickson would draw a client away from the detailed distractions of his problem and explore the deep-rooted cause. For his client the journey was one away from the specifics and towards the abstract. Much of this book is an example of my journey away from the specific (where I was, what I was doing) towards the abstract and conceptual (what I believe, who I am and why).

Leading someone along this same pathway will enable them to get in touch with the source of their motivation, indeed the source of their *being*. This model enables you to elicit reasons and answer the question, 'Why?'

The 'Meta Model' moves you in the other direction, from conceptual ideas and abstract thoughts through to specific implementation and implications. The model provides for a powerful way of eliciting information and answering the question, 'What, specifically?'

You will forgive me for not using these pages to teach these processes. Exploring the published work of Richard Bandler and John Grinder will provide you with far greater expertise.

With the right questions, asked in the right way at the right time, you can start to understand your own map of this world, as well as other people's maps, and how these maps may be limiting you in your dealings with business colleagues, partners or your children.

Outcomes

When I started to discover the magic, the wizardry of how to think, how to prompt with questions, how to mentor, how to coach, how to release in somebody a block in their thinking that may have been there for twenty or even thirty years, and just shift it out of the way for a second so that they gain a moment of in-sight, it led me right back to what had been my obsessions all through my life.

One of my obsessions had been conjuring. As a child I was fascinated by David Nixon's television programmes. He was my hero. Then I became fascinated from a hobby point of view by every aspect of conjuring. I could take a pack of cards, move my hand over the pack of cards, and the card on the top changed. I learned how to do these things. I started to earn my living conjuring and doing magic. This brought me to a career in the world of magic and illusion – theatre and television.

Now, as a coach I am guiding people towards making their own magic, their own transformations. I ask the question, and

I leave the question open. They go off into the 'real' world to find and live the solution. I do not give 'the' solution at the end of a session. What the Master did with Little Grasshopper was simply open a question in his mind. Once it was open the subconscious mind continued to seek resolution. As human beings we *have to* get to the resolution, we *have to* get to completion. So we do.

The wizardry in the Milton Model is the question, 'Why?' This is the question that gets to the heart of our purpose. It was only after we began building the business that we started to discover the whole purpose of the Institute of Human Development. With each question we asked ourselves we were not so much *designing* our purpose and our destiny, as *discovering* our purpose and our destiny.

Powerful questions produce answers that resonate deeply within you. I have learned to pay attention to that. I have learned to notice those questions and answers that produce an involuntary, physiological response. Those moments are signals that I am on to something which has a real meaning to me. All of the things that have excited me, and moved me to passion and moments of satori over the past five years, have all been to do with the magic of touching people's lives, the magic of drawing out of people something that they had forgotten was within them.

I was now experiencing, from my outer circle of influences to my inner circle of mentors, these moments on a regular basis. I can think of nothing more profound that I have experienced than these moments. I can think of nothing that has enabled me to burst through the boundaries of my own thinking, to crash through the limitations of my own career projection, to break through the glass ceilings of my finances, my relationships, my career more powerfully than simply those people having that magical ability to touch in with me and to ask me the questions that open me up to revelation and to understanding.

That was what the Institute was to be about.

Purpose and Passion

> *What is passion? It is surely the becoming of a person. Are we not, for most of our lives, marking time? Most of our being is at rest, unlived. In passion, the body and the spirit seek expression outside of self. Passion is all that is other from self. The more extreme and the more expressed that passion is, the more unbearable does life seem without it. It reminds us that if passion dies or is denied, we are partly dead and that soon, come what may, we will be wholly so.*
>
> JOHN BOORMAN

If I wanted to go on experiencing those moments, if I wanted to go on moving my career path forward, then, rather than deciding that I was a guru with all the answers, the consultant with all the solutions, I had to say, 'No, I am part of a process in which people consistently challenge, mentor, coach and guide each other on their journeys through their careers, through building their businesses, their lives and their relationships.'

The purpose of the Institute was to bring together the people best at this in the world, the people who had the most powerful ideas to teach, and the people who had the best skills at drawing out from individuals their own excellence. We were there to attract those people to the cause, to the mission, to the reason for being. The Institute was the formal structure that allowed for people, from whatever background or area of life they were in, but particularly from business, to say, 'If this magic is possible in a one-to-one relationship with people, then it can be transferred to teams and to groups. If that is possible it can be transferred to departments and organisations. If that is true then it can be transferred to communities and cultures.'

The Institute is about being an organisation that has within its walls people who coach other people through to a new level of excellence, of self-discovery, and self-realisation.

All of this had happened outside my conscious awareness. All of this had happened, to some extent, by accident. Yet, none of it could have happened without the learning experiences I have had, from my first day at school, from my first bad school report to a lifetime of bad reports, to a lifetime of operating outside people's expectations of me and of refusing to be conditioned by cultural hypnosis – 'Why can't you toe the line? . . . why can't you be like everybody else?' – and of refusing to be told what I can and can't do, what I must and mustn't do, and what is possible and what is not possible.

The Past – Taking the Guided Tour

I had discovered that there was a reason for my having encountered all of my relationship challenges in business, all of my financial challenges, and all of my operational challenges. Every single one of the businesses that I ran or was involved in had successes, and had failures. There was a reason for every one of those failures.

With the new skills that I was developing I was now able to look back at those failures and take the learnings, which had been available to me many, many years ago but which I had chosen to ignore or didn't have the tools to discover and listen to. I was able to go back, not just to my relationship with my former partners in the consultancy, but to every project that had been key, and draw out of it learning that meant that, having learned it, I am now better, more skilled, more capable, and more focused.

When you take a new meaning out of your past, you look back on a previous event, an event that used to mean something bad to you. That meaning then shaped the next few years of your life. When you are able to go back to that same event and find a new meaning, something good for you, you come back to where you are with a whole different history. You can see your history as *film noir*, as a series of repeating examples of people misunderstanding you, abusing your commitment, abusing your determination, benefiting from you, leaving you bruised and bleeding in the gutter; or you can go back and say, 'Every single one of those experiences was an opportunity to learn, and move forward and become stronger and more focused, become more talented and become more disciplined.' You have suddenly reinvented your history.

Wayne Dyer, one of America's most prolific and successful personal development authors, says it is never too late to have a happy childhood. Whatever the circumstances of your life and childhood, you can go on believing in your version, or you can go back and rewrite it. You can go back and say, 'My parents' behaviour didn't mean I wasn't loved, it meant they had not learned how to express love and affection; my husband's long and moody silences don't mean he is unhappy with me, they mean he needs time to sort out his own challenges and anxieties; the loss of my small child does not mean that God is cruel and has forgotten me, it means that God wanted her time to be pure, untroubled by life; my time in Auschwitz didn't mean that I had been rejected by my God and that, maybe, there was no God, it meant that I was there for a purpose.' You can go back and start to attach new meanings to each of those events. You can go back into your business and start to attach new meanings to the experiences of the successes and the failures and the missed opportunities that you have had.

There is no such thing as failure, if you go back, and take the learning out of it. It is only when you suppress the learning and ignore the opportunities in every eventuality that you miss out. It is only when you choose a life-draining meaning that you lose.

The only failure is refusing to stand up when you have been knocked down. That is my definition of failure. The only time that I will accept that word is when it means that somebody fell down and refused to stand up. Everything else, every standing up again, every opportunity to go back and learn again, is not a failure but a lesson, and a valuable lesson.

> *Defeat is not important. It is how you come back from defeat that is important.*
> ALEX FERGUSON, MANAGER, MANCHESTER
> UNITED FOOTBALL CLUB

The Future – A Rough Guide

The more willing you are to learn those lessons, the more willing you are to learn from those opportunities, the more willing you are to be honest about to what extent you are 'at cause' rather than 'at effect', that you are the catalyst rather than the victim, then the greater challenges you will be allowed, and the greater adventures you will be allowed to take part in. If you desire *that* adventure, you have to qualify for it. You have to qualify for it by achieving *this* adventure. If you refuse to learn the lessons from this adventure, if you refuse to move and to grow from this experience, then life tends to keep you from the next experience. You have to graduate.

If you cannot walk up a twelve-hundred-foot hill, then you will not be invited to climb Everest. There is something inside you that will protect you from the most dangerous slopes until you are ready, and equipped, and able to handle them. When you are able and equipped to handle them, you are *expected* to go. On the one hand life won't let you through the entrance gates until you've qualified; on the other, once you have qualified, life won't let you out again. You are expected to go up to the next level.

That is what your coaches and your mentors remind you of. They remind you of the expectation that you have of yourself, that other people have of you and, perhaps, that your purpose has of you. Whatever it is that you believe created you, or put you here, has an expectation of you that now obliges you to go to the next level.

While you refuse to go, you haven't learned the lesson. The things you fantasise about – the size of your business, the bottom-line profitability, the relationship with a loved one, what you want for your children – those things will be denied you, or delayed until you are willing to learn the current lesson, the current task that you have been set. Hercules could not move on to destroying the Boar of Erymanthus or the Stymphalian Birds, until he had armoured himself with the skin he had taken from the Nemean Lion. If he had refused to face the Lion of Nemea, there would have been no other victories. He couldn't have continued his quest on to the next adventure.

In George Lucas' breathtaking film series of *Star Wars*, Luke Skywalker is warned by Yoda not to face Darth Vader until he has mastered The Force. Only when he has mastered that, is he ready to meet the destiny that is awaiting him.

In Disney's *The Lion King*, Simba lives years of 'carefree' irresponsibility in the company of his purposeless friends before facing magical and life-changing questioning by Nala about his identity and his purpose. What follows is a magnificent portrayal of inner turmoil as the lion comes face to face with what lies dormant within him. 'You are more than you have become,' he is told by the memory of his father. Facing his past is painful and powerful; it brings him face to face with who he is and why he must return to his kingdom and reclaim the throne.

In his masterpiece, *The Hero with a Thousand Faces*, Joseph Campbell tells us how this unifying tale of self-discovery – this inner process of personal revelation – has been told again and again and again through the characters of Apollo, Wotan, Buddha and countless fairytales, myths and legends from every culture that has lived under the sun.

These stories of self-discovery and heroic quests have been told to us for generations for a reason. If we strip away the personalities of the individual heroes in these tales – the cultural dressings that come from East and West, North and South – we discover a consistent message which must be pointing towards a simple, universal truth about the nature of life and our rôle in it. These stories cry out, 'Pay attention! There is a reason!'

Here I am. I think I am looking at Peak Performance Coaching in twentieth-century psychology, and what am I learning? I am learning lessons that Socrates gave us, that Virgil and Homer gave us, that the Vedic sages gave us, that Disney gave us, that Spielberg and Lucas are giving us. Moses, Jesus, Mohammed, Lao Tzu, the Aborigines and North American natives have been telling the story for thousands of years, and that story is the same one, in different costumes – over and over again. It is the story of the hero who turns his gaze from the outside and looks inside for the pathway to his destiny and the courage to embrace it.

> *We've all been taught to look outside ourselves for sustenance – to look beyond the self . . . for fulfilment . . . but it's possible to reverse our gaze from outward to inward. And when we do, we find an energy we've . . . not previously identified.*
>
> DR WAYNE DYER

The story will go on being told as long as there are people wanting to hear and willing to listen.

There is a reason!

16: OASIS

Life is either a daring adventure or nothing.

HELEN KELLER

*L*ooking back over this book I had all sorts of emotional responses to it. One was 'It's almost unbelievable what has been happening over the last five years' another was 'How unexceptional my story is, compared with many of the unstoppable people I have been hearing about, or listening to, or reading about.'

Before I had the courage to publish this book I had to ask myself, 'What is its reason, what is this book here for?' The best place to find the answer was where we started. Remember the second traveller to cross the desert, walking in the footsteps of somebody who had been before him, and drinking at the wells that someone else had dug? I would not have been able to make a single one of the steps I have taken were it not that largely I have been following in the footsteps of people who have been before me.

Sometimes I have found that I have been following a path that turned out not to be right for me, but then I have been able to retrace my steps for a while and follow another path, another teacher, another guide. All the time I am treading in the path that has been laid for me. If, by writing this book, I can dig some of the wells a little deeper, or make some other footprints for you to follow, then I will have achieved my purpose.

The most important reminder, for me, is that unstoppable people are not exceptional people. They are ordinary people, doing ordinary things, so exceptionally well that it gives them an energy and a momentum that makes them unstoppable. When they connect with their dream, and when they decide to cross the threshold and take part in the quest, they release a power that cannot be diminished by delay and disappointment.

Crossing the threshold, taking that first step, is the hardest. Standing at the edge of the desert, remembering everything they have taught you at school about how wide this desert is, how hot it will be, how few resources there will be, how little water there is, is why so many fail to take that first step. But those are not the thoughts I allow into my head as I stand at the edge of the desert. I fill my head with the stories of the people who have done it. I remember those who have stepped into the heat and pressed ahead. I see pictures of other adventurers – sometimes striding, sometimes stumbling, but always continuing to live their dream.

What, then, are the differences between the people who turn away and the people who make that journey? This book may answer that question for you. Maybe this book will be one more piece of the jigsaw for you, as you explore your own quest. It certainly doesn't promise to offer a complete map for your journey, but it does offer to point you in the direction of a number of unstoppable people who can help you to become unstoppable as you pursue your own vision.

The book is also a reminder to me of how, with each leg of this journey completed and successfully behind me, I am faced with what seems a much steeper hill and a much rougher rock face to climb. Somehow I know that the previous leg of the journey has given me the skills and the stamina to make the climb, and the belief that, however this journey turns out, I shall be equipped to deal with it. As I climb this hill, ford that stream, or face another glacier, I know that somewhere in my mind and somewhere in my spirit will be the resources that I need to move on.

As the journey continues I do not expect the challenges to become any fewer or any less intense. Quite the reverse: as I grow and as I develop and as I mature, I expect the universe to present me with greater challenges, not lesser ones. That is exciting, sometimes frightening, but always thrilling.

From the temporary oasis I have reached, at the end of this particular leg of the journey, at the end of this particular book, I have a moment to pause, and look back and ask, what is it that made the difference between each of those moments where I was struggling, and each of those moments where I was able to make a leap forward? I look back at the people I have met whom I allowed to hinder my journey, and who are hindering their own; and the people I have met who are unstoppable in the pursuit of their dreams. What is the difference?

Their journeys are all individual and the paths they choose to follow unique, but for all of them there is more than just a belief in their dream. For all of them there is a profound sense of certainty, that holds within it room for doubt; one of the great human paradoxes that I ponder all the time. There is an absolute certainty that in the moment their dream is the right dream, and room for doubt that they are necessarily on the right path.

If I look at the businesses that I have had the opportunity to work in, and the opportunity to study, and if I look at the business leaders that I have had the pleasure and privilege to meet, the ones that stick in my mind are not those with the most charisma. Nor are they those with the greatest intellect, nor the greatest accumulation of wealth.

They are the ones with the greatest concentration of passion about what they do.

I think of Charles Dunstone, building up the Carphone Warehouse; Julian Richer building up Richer Sounds; Anita Roddick creating the Body Shop – an organisation not just committed to retail, but committed to changing the world;

Richard Branson, whose hobbies and personal pursuits as well as his business pursuits are full of a passion that is infectious; Fred Smith, Michael Basch and the founding team of Federal Express who, against odds that most of us can only have nightmares about, fuelled that company, not with money but with passion and belief and a sense of certainty that they were right; the great athletes; Nelson Mandela; Mahatma Gandhi; Kathy Buckley; Joseph Jaworski, and the hundreds who have inspired me with their tales of commitment.

The one thing that all these people have in common is not their personal style, nor their interpersonal skills, nor their business skills, but their passion, and their determination to listen silently, so that when, at the still point, the call for their particular quest came, they were listening for the call.

What distinguishes them is their absolute certainty, their absolute integrity. Gandhi, Buddha, Krishna, Christ *were*, Mandela and so many of the others who inspire us *are* what they believe. That is why thousands followed them then, and follow them now.

Listening to that inner voice they gained a clarity of understanding of *why* they were here, of *what legacy* it was they were to leave behind, and *for what reason* it was that they had the experiences they had. Unstoppable people are willing to hear that voice, pay attention to it and, having *listened*, develop the resources of character within themselves to say, 'Yes, I hear the call and I am coming. I see the challenge and I am prepared to meet it.'

What *is* it that these people have?

They have a passion and an unshakeable faith.

Passion

> *Men are only truly great when they act from the passions.*
> BENJAMIN DISRAELI

Where does that passion come from?

I am not sure I know where it comes from, but I am beginning to discover how to access it, and how to guide other people to the point where they access it. It is something to do with having the courage to take the first step, against all the overwhelming evidence that the world will present for *not* taking the first step. It comes from the courage to step into the future with nothing to depend on but faith – the faith that you are being drawn in the right direction, at the right time, in the right way, against all the crowding reasons that others will give you for not taking that step, for not making that journey.

The passion comes, then, from listening to yourself describe the things that matter most to you in your life, these values that become the boundaries of your journey, which sketch out the outline of the pathways for you. If you are clear about your values, about what matters to you, about the way that you would like to be seen living your life, the marker posts mapping the way are clear to you. If you follow that pathway, within those values, those key principles that you, in your heart, have established, you will find yourself on the right road.

The passion comes from a belief, a faith, a certainty that comes to you when you are operating within those beliefs about people, about the world, about what is possible and what is not possible, about who you are and why you are here.

The passion comes from that clarity about *you*, and about how you describe yourself, and how you want to be described, that sense of self that fuels your confidence and your courage.

The passion comes from asking yourself questions that will produce answers that are not always very comfortable: questions such as 'If I knew that I couldn't possibly fail, what would I choose to do with the rest of my life?' 'What is the legacy I want to leave behind?' 'Beyond "me" and my own material and emotional needs, who or what am I serving on this journey?'

When you start to ask those questions, you start to build a passion and an energy inside yourself that will move you over and beyond any of the hurdles, any of the delays that present themselves. This is something that I am only beginning to experience as I take these first few steps on my own particular journey, on my own particular quest. I am able to take those steps because I am willing to listen to others who have been before me, to look at the maps that others have drawn, to use the tools that others have used, to follow the pathways that others have followed. I am ready to seek out as my mentors other unstoppable people to guide me in different moments on that path. I connect with their passion, their energy, their belief systems. I allow them to stretch me, to push me, to open up for me dreams and visions and ideas of what is possible and what is desirable and what needs to be done.

Why This Book?

This book began at the point where my world was collapsing around me. It moved on to my recognising some of the skills and capabilities I had acquired from my many challenges and experiences, not least looking at 'failure' in a new light and knowing what questions to ask of myself. It has recorded the moments when I was invited to ask the question, 'What matters to me now? Bearing in mind my history and my background, what are my values and my beliefs?' It has mapped out my search for a sense of identity, a sense of self, and watched me find some resonance in the rôle of a guide. It has enabled me to explore a vision of a quest and think about the journey on which I have embarked.

Now it is time to ask, *Why* is this book?

Unstoppable People is about the nature of serving. It is serving something that lies outside Adrian Gilpin. It is about laying down yet more pathways for other people to explore. Magnificent pathways have been made available to me by strangers who are along the road, ahead of me. These pathways have enabled me to achieve what I would never have been able to achieve without their guidance.

When you discover that this is what other people have been doing for you, perhaps there is an obligation to make the pathways available to others. I believe your task is to speak of these things in your own voice, in your own special way, in order to attract those people who may be attracted by what you have to say. It is not your task to convince those who are not interested, who do not respond to you, but simply to attract those who are drawn by your tone of voice and your way of describing these things.

Your task is to put the significance that you have drawn down from your teachers and your mentors into a language that *you* understand, so that *you* can undertake the journey with vigour and a renewed sense of certainty. Then you will find that there are other people out there who will respond to your voice, and learn for themselves the great joy of playing their part in this unfolding and continuous odyssey.

I am gradually beginning to be able to articulate some sense of my own purpose. When you start to do this, it is strange and self-conscious. The language that comes to mind can be imprecise, uncertain, even a little embarrassing as you grasp at ways to describe who you are. In time you find a language that will feel more congruent, as the images become more vivid, and something happens in your heart. When eventually you do find the right words, you feel your spirit soar.

For me a consistent image has been emerging, quite like the image in a photograph appearing slowly on the paper as it swims beneath the surface of the liquid developer. It is the image of a figure standing at the edge of a stream taking the hand of other travellers and guiding them across the stepping stones; someone reaching out when a boat comes to dock and supporting the passengers as they step to the shore; someone standing at the bottom of the mountain and helping climbers up the first few steps, then being at the top of the mountain as they make the final push, always guiding the traveller to where they want to be. I see myself as that person – offering the hand across the river, up the mountain, down the glacier, because other people have offered me their hands, have given me phenomenal opportunities, have been there for me. When you think about you, what images come to mind, how do you describe yourself and your rôle?

At first this growing sense of purpose presented itself to me in very abstract and esoteric terms. I heard it for a long time, and argued with it, and refused to make the journey, and rejected the call. I busied myself with money-making, busied myself with business-building, busied myself with all sorts of other activities to quieten down the voice that I was beginning to hear. I heard it for a long time until, having *listened* to it at last, now I am becoming clearer and clearer about precisely what it is that I want to achieve. A chance discovery of a handful of words spoken to playwright Václav Havel by the Czech philosopher and activist Jan Patocka resonated in my heart as I was thinking about this chapter. '*The real test of a man is not how well he plays the rôle he has invented for himself, but how well he plays the rôle that destiny assigned to him.*'

What I am encountering now is the big 'Why?' that is coming, it seems, from outside me. It is coming from a voice that is not entirely mine. I do not know where it is from. I have no way of describing where it is from, but I am listening to it.

As I write about this something very strange happens deep inside me. These images of guiding, these thoughts of discovering a purpose, a reason for being me, are very powerful and often very unsettling. It is uncomfortable, too, having to put the thoughts into words for public view. What is the purpose of speaking and writing about these intimate things?

Perhaps it is this. When I coach individuals, privately and in seminars, through processes which help them articulate a sense of self and a sense of purpose I see a magical transformation take place in their spirit. A sense of self and a sense of purpose reside in all of us. So often we sense these thoughts of self and purpose within us, but resist the language and the images that come to mind, perhaps because of their simplicity.

So often, particularly with business people, these processes can initially be greeted with reserve and resistance. When I have the privilege to talk to great business leaders, however, there is no such inhibition; they speak freely of their vision and purpose. It is the simplicity and the humanity and the obviousness of the ways that they describe these things that give them their power – power to rekindle the flame of certainty in their own spirit, and power to attract followers and companions.

Recently, as Britain was plodding through an interminable general election campaign, the leader of the Labour party, Tony Blair, was making regular election broadcasts on national radio comparing the great diversity of Britain's talents and cultures to individual players in an orchestra making music. He wanted the electorate to see him as a conductor bringing all the players and instruments together in harmony, making individual talent all the more potent as it was harnessed into a single, magnificent concert sound. The metaphor was powerful and part of what attracted the electorate. Only time will tell if he is able to create the harmonies he believes in.

There are great leaders who see themselves as standard-bearers leading the troops, teachers drawing out excellence from their followers, magicians turning pounds and dollars into millions, priests serving the growth of their people, fathers guiding the hands of their children, mothers nurturing life and talent in theirs, mavericks creating new futures, wizards transforming ideas into products, or warriors fighting a battle for supremacy. With each metaphor comes a powerful energy that drives the leader through delays and over hurdles.

In my experience, we start this process by choosing the images and language of identity and purpose wisely. Then we must allow our subconscious to reshape the images and re-work the language until our heart and spirit are moved. When you have found a way to articulate your own sense of being you will feel it in your body – your heart will beat faster or your stomach will churn or the hair on the back of your neck will bristle; somewhere inside you will know that you have found a way to speak of these things. It will almost certainly be like a rush of adrenaline; an inspiring flow of emotional energy.

Perhaps the deeper purpose of this book is to inspire you to give yourself permission to explore, discover and articulate these things for yourself. Others gave me the opportunity to do this and this is my way of making their gift available to others. I have stepped into the footsteps of others in order to find my own path and I have drunk at the wells that others have dug when I have been thirsty. My journey has become easier for riding on the shoulders of giants, and I will travel further for it. There are giants willing to hold you high; you will find them. Look for them; you will travel further with them than on your own.

Serving people's journeys of self-discovery has become the guiding purpose of the Institute of Human Development.

*There is not accident in our choice of reading. All
our sources are related.*

FRANÇOIS MAURIAC

If this book can describe things in a tone of voice that resonates with *you*, then you, the reader, are beginning to hear the same call to your own quest. Ask yourself why this book has come into your hands right now. Ask, 'Why am I responding to some of the things that are being said in this book?' Ask yourself what brought you to the end, for only a few of you who pick up this book will have come to the end. A tiny percentage of the people who have bought or been given this book will read to this chapter. Why have *you* read this far?

It is not because I am offering you some universal truth. There may be a single truth out there, but if there is it has to be described in a million different ways. It is simply that I am offering you some stepping stones in a language that is resonating with you. Hear that voice, and learn how to listen to it. Learn how to touch in with your own sense of values, realign your beliefs, understand who you are and why you are here. Trust the voice.

I am so grateful to Marianne Williamson, the author of *A Return to Love* and a magnificent teacher, for permission to bring this book to an end with her words, words that I have quoted before in this book and which I have often heard attributed to Nelson Mandela and to other great leaders – a small sign of her impact on the world. These words should lie in the hearts of all those who are called to lead organisations, societies, communities, nations and families:

*Our deepest fear is not that we are inadequate. Our deepest fear is that
we are powerful beyond measure. It is our light, not our darkness, that
most frightens us. We ask ourselves, Who am I to be brilliant, gorgeous,*

*talented, fabulous? Actually who are you **not** to be? You are a child of God. Your playing small doesn't serve the world. There's nothing enlightened about shrinking so that other people won't feel insecure around you. We are all meant to shine, as children do. As we let our own light shine, we unconsciously give other people permission to do the same. As we're liberated from our own fear, our presence automatically liberates others.*

If this book achieves its purpose, if it liberates you to shine, by any degree, then the unstoppable people who have been, and continue to be, part of my life, are talking to you, too.

They are inviting you to join them.

Recommended Reading

TEAM DEVELOPMENT

Dr Stephen R. Covey, *The 7 Habits of Highly Effective People*, Simon & Schuster

Dr Stephen R. Covey, *Principle-Centered Leadership*, Simon & Schuster

Two of the most influential American books on personal effectiveness. Something of an evangelist, Dr Covey can be a bit prescriptive but his work is accessible, intelligent, and he is one of my favourite teachers. A Master who walks his talk.

Charles Handy, *The Empty Raincoat*, Arrow Books

Charles Handy, *Beyond Certainty*, Arrow Books

The UK's best writer about the changing face of organisations and the attitudes and skills needed to cope.

Peter Senge, *Fifth Discipline*, Century

Senge's masterwork on the Learning Organisation

Peter Senge, *The Fifth Discipline Fieldbook*, Nicholas Brealey

Great, if somewhat unstructured, series of essays on organisational learning. Becoming a bible for Human Resources (HR) and Training directors. No one is doing more innovative work in organisational learning than Senge and his colleagues at MIT.

Ken Blanchard and Others, *One-Minute Manager* books, HarperCollins

This ever-growing series of books has become legendary. Blanchard realised that on average only about 7 per cent of a business book gets read before it starts to gather dust. So he writes books that are about 7 per cent of the length of business books. Result – people read his books to the end. A great teacher, and a pretty good businessman, it seems.

PERSONAL DEVELOPMENT

Anthony Robbins, *Unlimited Power*, Simon & Schuster
Anthony Robbins, *Awaken The Giant Within*, Simon & Schuster
Probably America's most flamboyant personal-development guru, and his seminars are something of a stretch for a UK audience. However, no one can deny Robbins' extraordinary genius at making highly complex subjects accessible to all. He is probably one of the world's most skilful communicators and coaches many celebrity athletes and entertainers.

Napoleon Hill, *Think and Grow Rich*, Hawthorn Books Inc., New York
The book that started it all – at least this century! Still relevant and surprisingly contemporary.

Ian McDermott and Joseph O'Connor, *Practical NLP for Managers*, Gower
Ian is one of the very few teachers of Neuro-Linguistic Programming (NLP) who gets it right, makes it practical and persuades his pupils to live by the principles rather than work the techniques. A good book to introduce business managers to the principles.

Sue Knight, *NLP at Work*, Nicholas Brealey
A very concise and intelligent introduction to the subject of Neuro-Linguistic Programming. Sue seems to be one of the few NLP writers who really understands business and leadership.

Robert Dilts, *Changing Belief Systems with NLP*, Meta Publications
Complex, academic work about the structure of belief systems. Brilliant work for the dedicated student.

Daniel Goleman, *Emotional Intelligence*, Bloomsbury Publishing
You can't have missed the bookshop displays over Christmas 1996. A book that argues that success and excellence are not about intelligence (IQ) but about how we master our emotional experiences. I can't disagree! Goleman makes all this easy to grasp.

LEADERSHIP AND ORGANISATIONAL DEVELOPMENT

Joseph Jaworski, *Synchronicity – The Inner Path of Leadership*, Berrett-Koehler
Simply the finest book I have read in twenty years. It is about leadership, personal fulfilment and creating a world to which I would like to belong. For thousands of years mankind has known that human fulfilment comes from exploring an *inner* process of discovery. Writers from every spiritual tradition have tried to make this accessible. Jaworski simply tells it as it is for him. A moving, inspiring and emotionally draining read. This book will lead the vanguard in redefining what it is that makes a leader.

Robert Dilts, *Visionary Leadership Skills*, Meta Publications
Robert's book is based on his experience of modelling leadership skills at Fiat and later at IBM. His loyalty and commitment to the field of NLP which he has helped to pioneer are creditable, but may be keeping his work from a wider audience which he greatly deserves.

Margaret Wheatley, *Leadership and the New Science*, Berrett-Koehler

A pioneering book presenting the work on the new quantum scientists in a format that makes you rethink the leadership agenda. Vital, if slightly stodgy, reading for anyone who wants to explore the theory which lies beneath Jaworski's book (above).

Julian Richer, *The Richer Way*, EMAP

For six consecutive years Julian Richer's company Richer Sounds has achieved the highest sales per square foot of any retail business globally. He has built a £50 million group of companies from scratch. How? Largely through an exceptional attitude to people – customers, colleagues and suppliers. This book tells you precisely how he achieves his success. Phenomena – Julian *and* his book!

James C. Collins and Jerry I. Porras, *Built to Last*, Century

The highly readable result of a massive research project done at Stanford University into what makes a visionary company. 'Collins and Porras will emerge as the gurus to watch over the next decade.' IOD *Director* magazine

Leaders of commercial organisations cannot afford to pass this book by. It challenges many existing beliefs about successful businesses, and will be a painful read for some. Many will deny its findings and opinions; a few will use it to catalyse radical change in their fortunes.

Edward de Bono, *Tactics – The Art and Science of Success*, HarperCollins

Based on a series of interviews with men and women who have achieved extraordinary success. De Bono brings his ingenious mind to the task of analysing the radically different mindsets of successful people.

Ricardo Semler, *Maverick,* **Arrow Books**
The most extraordinary example of what is possible in a business where the rules have not been tweaked but rewritten. Restores your faith in possibility and it's a great book to fling at MBAs when they start to irritate you.

Ken Lewis and Stephen Lytton, *How to Transform Your Company and Enjoy It!* **Management Books 2000 Ltd**
Unlikely to become a bestseller, which is a shame. A real example of business enlightenment in a medium-sized engineering firm in Bedfordshire. Buy it in preference to any of the theoretical textbooks. If you want a conference speaker who tells it as it is – Ken Lewis is brilliant.

Mike Davidson, *The Grand Strategist,* **Macmillan**
Short (which means I managed to read it). So much appalling balderdash is written about strategy that it appealed to me that someone had got the principles down into a few pages! Owes a great debt to the style of Ken Blanchard's *One-Minute Manager* books, and worth a visit.

MIND SKILLS and LEARNING TOOLS
Tony Buzan, *The Mind Map Book,* **BBC Books**
Quite brilliant! I wish I did more of this. For those who want to maximise their thinking and learning skills, Buzan is your man. *The Mind Map Book* is probably the one that will get you started on mind gym. Mind Maps really will transform your ability to take memorable notes and your ability to plan complex projects, books or presentations.

Edward de Bono, *Textbook of Wisdom,* **Viking**
Fun. Intriguing. I'd love to be on this wavelength.

Colin Rose and Louise Goll, *Accelerate Your Learning*, Accelerated Learning Systems Ltd, Aylesbury, Bucks.

Accelerated learning is a series of techniques developed out of the original work of Dr Howard Gardner of Harvard University. Well worth a look. You may have seen this company's language-learning products advertised in the newspapers and supplements. Great for helping children and unstructured learners like me.

THE INNER GAME

Joseph Jaworski, *Synchronicity – The Inner Path of Leadership*

See comments above under Leadership and Organisational Development.

Fritjof Capra, *The Web of Life*, Flamingo

An extraordinary work that synthesises new developments in science, philosophy and human spirituality. Dr Capra is one of the leading contemporary commentators on the nature and essence of human life. Much more accessible than the subject-matter sounds.

Dan Millman, *Way of the Peaceful Warrior*, H. J. Kramer (California)

Highly original, provocative, humorous and spiritual novel based very firmly on Dan Millman's own life and journey of self-discovery. This is a book that can answer many deep questions about the nature of personal mastery and that has helped to change many people's lives.

Dr Wayne Dyer, *Your Sacred Self*, HarperCollins

Dr Dyer reigns supreme in the field of deep personal development and fulfilment in America. His work is developing a dedicated readership in Britain and his seminars are life-enhancing. Most famous for his book *Erroneous Zones*, in this particular work he takes his thinking further and deeper.

Dr Deepak Chopra, *The Seven Spiritual Laws of Success*, Bantam Books
Dr Chopra's work is for those who are on or seeking an inner journey. He has combined Eastern philosophy, Western medicine and the new sciences in a lifetime of talking and writing about the nature of humanity and what lies beyond. A student of Maharishi Mahesh Yogi (guru to the Beatles), he is now a guru in his own right and is rarely out of the media's gaze. Unique, thought-provoking material. He has published many other books on health and reversing the ageing process.

Dr Deepak Chopra, *Creating Affluence*, New World Library, California
Dr Chopra applies his philosophy to creating wealth.

George S. Clayson, *The Richest Man in Babylon*, Signet
A classic parable about wealth creation. A three-hour read. Excellent. Whole careers have been founded on teaching the principles that are embedded within this book.

Joseph Campbell, *The Hero with a Thousand Faces*, Fontana
'Campbell's words carry extraordinary weight, not only among scholars but among a wide range of other people who find his search down mythical pathways relevant to their lives today.' *Time* magazine.
   A magnificent tour of myth and fable from every corner of the globe – and the messages are all the same.

Nelson Mandela, *Long Walk to Freedom*, Abacus

A long read, too. One of the most important political books of our generation and one that demonstrates the human being's capacity to transcend suffering. This book will electrify anyone who believes that transformational leadership must be built on faith and purpose. It is about the unlimited power of the human spirit.

Marianne Williamson, *A Return to Love,* Thorsons

A very special book to guide spiritual development. While rooted in the Christian philosophy of *A Course in Miracles,* it is widely read by people from many different cultural and spiritual traditions. In a way this is its own miracle; it speaks to many different people.

THE INSTITUTE OF HUMAN DEVELOPMENT

SHORT BUSINESS PRESENTATIONS
We run a number of short (1- to 2½-hour) presentations on various aspects of our curriculum. These are available for:

Large Businesses   Training and Enterprise Councils
Professional Networks   Mentor Groups
Membership   Special-Interest Groups
   Associations

Presentations can be developed from our curriculum. Examples include:

* The Reality Gap – **The Gap between What You Want and What You Are Getting**
* Unstoppable Leaders – **Attracting and Motivating Willing Followers**
* Transformation: Leading the Way Forward **Beyond Incremental Change into Corporate Transformation**
* Quantum Selling – **Capturing the Heart and Mind of the Customer**

FULL DEVELOPMENT PROGRAMMES
We offer a full range of development programmes to organisations wishing to manage their growth through the development of their people.

CORPORATE SUPPORT
The IHD will support you at all levels throughout your change- and development-programmes. We will provide coaching and support for chief executives through to training programmes

for managers and junior colleagues, cascading a common language of achievement throughout the organisation.

For full details of our consultants and speakers please contact:
>   The Institute of Human Development
>   Freepost, Tonbridge, Kent, TN11 8BR, England
>   Free Phone: 0800 074 0518   Free Fax: 0800 074 0519

THE TRANSFORMATIONAL
LEADERSHIP FORUM

The TLF is a high-level global network of business leaders, academics, thinkers and advisers who collectively explore the emerging models of leadership that can impact successful organisational change.

Membership is by invitation. If you are interested in participating in research, conferences, dialogue and workshops with some of the world's leading thinkers and practitioners in leadership, please tell us of your interest.

There are three equal-status categories of membership:

Founder Members – open to major sponsors and research partners;

Corporate Members – open to organisations and individuals who have a passionate interest in the emerging models of leadership excellence and who want easy access to the best practical development work being done in this field. Members participate in learning forums where they share their experiences of challenges and solutions to pioneering business excellence;

Faculty Members – leading consultants, academics and facilitators who specialise in leadership and team development. Faculty Members are invited to cascade, test and debate their ideas and experience with highly experienced and senior business leaders.

For full details please contact:
The Institute of Human Development
Freepost, Tonbridge, Kent, TN11 8BR, England
Phone Free on 0800 074 0518
Fax Free on 0800 074 0519